Physical Characteristics of the American Water Spaniel

(from the American Kennel Club breed standard)

Body: Well-developed, sturdily constructed but not too compactly coupled. Well-developed brisket extending to elbow. The ribs well-sprung. The loins strong.

Hindquarters: Well-developed hips and thighs with the whole rear assembly showing strength and drive. The hock joint slightly rounded, moderately angulated. Legs from hock joint to foot pad moderate in length, strong and straight with good bone structure. Hocks parallel.

Tail: Moderate in length, curved in a rocker fashion, can be carried either slightly below or above the level of the back. The tail is tapered, lively and covered with hair with moderate feathering.

Size: 15 to 18 inches for either sex. Males weighing 30–45 lbs. Females weighing 25–40 lbs.

Coat: Can range from marcel (uniform waves) to closely curled. The amount of waves or curls can vary from one area to another on the dog. It is important to have undercoat to provide sufficient density to be of protection against weather, water or punishing cover, yet not too coarse or too soft. The throat, neck and rear of the dog well-covered with hair. The ear well-covered with hair on both sides with ear canal evident upon inspection. Forehead covered with short smooth hair and without topknot. Tail covered with hair to tip with moderate feathering. Legs have moderate feathering with waves or curls to harmonize with coat of dog. Coat may be trimmed to present a well groomed appearance; the ears may be shaved; but neither is required.

Color: Either solid liver, brown or dark chocolate. A little white on toes and chest permissible.

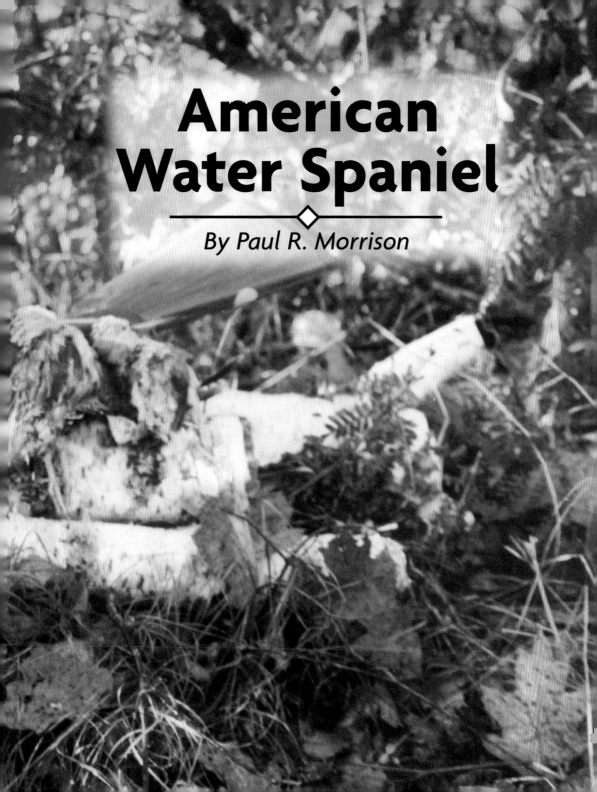

American Water Spaniel

◇

By Paul R. Morrison

Contents

8   **History of the** American Water Spaniel

Dive into the origins of this versatile and endearing water spaniel. Also known as "America's Own," the American Water Spaniel shares the company of very few breeds developed in the United States. As you trace the ancestry of this delightful hunter and companion, meet the determined founder of the breed, Dr. F. J. "Doc" Pfeifer, and other people and dogs instrumental in the breed's establishment.

26 **Characteristics of the** American Water Spaniel

The American Water Spaniel loves to be the center of attention whether in the field, show ring or home and is quite impressive in all three arenas. See what makes the AWS so versatile and why it is equally respected in both the field and the home. With a penchant for hearing its own voice and a size that won't "tip the boat," learn whether or not the AWS is for you.

36 **Breed Standard for the** American Water Spaniel

Learn the requirements of a well-bred American Water Spaniel by studying the description of the breed set forth in the American Kennel Club standard. Both show dogs and pets must possess key characteristics as outlined in the breed standard.

44   **Your Puppy** American Water Spaniel

Find out about how to locate a well-bred American Water Spaniel puppy. Discover which questions to ask the breeder and what to expect when visiting the litter. Prepare for your puppy-accessory shopping spree. Also discussed are home safety, the first trip to the vet, socialization and solving basic puppy problems.

68 **Proper Care of Your** American Water Spaniel

Cover the specifics of taking care of your American Water Spaniel every day: feeding for the puppy, adult and senior dog; grooming, including coat care, ears, eyes, nails and bathing; and exercise needs for your dog. Also discussed are the essentials of dog ID, safe travel with your dog and boarding.

Training Your American Water Spaniel 88

Begin with the basics of training the puppy and adult dog. Learn the principles of house-training the American Water Spaniel, including the use of crates and basic scent instincts. Get started by introducing the pup to his collar and leash and progress to the basic commands. Find out about obedience classes and training for water sports.

Healthcare of Your American Water Spaniel 111

By Lowell Ackerman DVM, DACVD
Become your dog's healthcare advocate and a well-educated canine keeper. Select a skilled and able veterinarian. Discuss pet insurance, vaccinations and infectious diseases, the neuter/spay decision and a sensible, effective plan for parasite control, including fleas, ticks and worms.

Your Senior American Water Spaniel 134

Know when to consider your American Water Spaniel a senior and what special needs he will have. Learn to recognize the signs of aging in terms of physical and behavioral traits and what your vet can do to optimize your dog's golden years. Consider some advice about saying goodbye to your beloved pet.

Showing Your American Water Spaniel 140

Step into the center ring and find out about the world of showing pure-bred dogs. Here's how to get started in AKC shows, how they are organized and what's required for your dog to become a champion. Take a leap into the realms of obedience and field trials, agility and hunting tests.

Index 156

KENNEL CLUB BOOKS® AMERICAN WATER SPANIEL
ISBN: 1-59378-411-2

Copyright © 2007 • Kennel Club Books® • A Division of BowTie, Inc.
40 Broad Street, Freehold, NJ 07728 USA
Cover Design Patented: US 6,435,559 B2 • Printed in South Korea

Library of Congress Cataloging-in-Publication Data
Morrison, Paul R.
  American water spaniel / by Paul R. Morrison.
    p. cm. -- (A Comprehensive owner's guide)
  ISBN 1-59378-411-2
  1. American water spaniel. I. Title.
  SF429.A735M67 2007
  636.752'4-dc22   2006029192
      10 9 8 7 6 5 4 3 2 1

Photography by Isabelle Français and Juliette Cunliffe
with additional photos by:

Mary Bloom, Paulette Braun, Alan and Sandy Carey, Carolina Biological Supply, Tom DiGiacomo, Karen Giles, Stephen Hall, Carol Ann Johnson, Bill Jonas, Dr. Dennis Kunkel, Ludwig Photography, Tam C. Nguyen, Phototake, Jean Claude Revy, Sanne Rutloh, Jay Singh, Luis Sosa, Susan and Lennah, Chuck Tatham and Christina Timbury.

Illustrations by Patricia Peters.

AMERICAN WATER SPANIEL

Known as America's Own, a Yankee Doodle Dandy, the Forgotten American and many other labels placed upon it by writers of yesterday and today, the American Water Spaniel shares the company of only a few breeds developed in the United States. Its history is steeped in lore that sometimes proclaims it to have been on the first ships to discover North America or to have been a part of Native American communities before the Europeans learned of its great abilities. While the truth will never be fully known it is more likely that a less romantic, albeit far from humdrum past, surrounds the AWS.

A proud AWS owner with a day's bag circa 1930s.

Chroniclers of this spaniel's history take its origin back to the mid-19th century, sometime around the Civil War days, and place its area of origin in the upper Midwest, specifically parts of Wisconsin known as the Wolf and Fox River Valleys. While this location and time cannot be proven, it is a pretty safe bet that this indeed is the time and place of the AWS's development. No matter where one places the birth of the AWS, it is an accepted claim that the breed developed from the needs of the market hunters of the day.

Market hunters were a rugged group who earned at least part of their living by harvesting large numbers of waterfowl and upland game for sale in local markets and restaurants. In the upper Midwest such men would work the marshes, lakes, river valleys and countryside in pursuit of game. Travel to the hunting areas was not necessarily done by car, train or even wagon but instead by skiff and canoe. These small craft were not conducive to ferrying a man, his hunting gear, the day's take and a big dog, so small dogs that would not overturn the boat when working yet worked tirelessly were prized by the hunters.

In the market-hunting era, it was not unusual for such hunters to harvest dozens of waterfowl at a time. Such large harvests left many birds lying in cover where they were difficult to spot or find, and it took the work of a good dog to ferret such birds out of thick cattails, reed beds and the surrounding land. Accomplishing such work required a dog to have a good nose to locate its quarry, a thick and water-repellent coat to maintain warmth and shed water and a hearty disposition to work all day long if need be. Additionally the dog would be expected to pull double duty and stand guard over the harvest, protecting it from other animals and some of the hunter's unscrupulous competitors.

Market hunters were an independent lot that seem to have preferred making their living by utilizing nature's bounty. It was not unusual for some of these folk

PURE-BRED PURPOSE

Given the vast range of the world's 400 or so pure breeds of dog, it's fair to say that domestic dogs are the most versatile animal in the kingdom. From the tiny 1-pound lap dog to the 200-pound guard dog, dogs have adapted to every need and whim of their human masters. Humans have selectively bred dogs to alter physical attributes like size, color, leg length, mass and skull diameter in order to suit our own needs and fancies. Dogs serve humans not only as companions and guardians but also as hunters, exterminators, shepherds, rescuers, messengers, warriors, babysitters and more!

to also use trapping as a source of their income and, by some accounts, more than a few of them used a dog for tracking down quarry that escaped their traps and for catching what author David Duffey once referred to as "runner rats." These were muskrats that moved across the frozen water of marshes right after the first freeze. Dogs were used to snatch these animals from the ice and return them to the trapper. A big dog would have trouble on the fragile ice and a timid dog would balk at doing battle with a muskrat fighting for its very existence. Dogs light in weight, swift of foot and tenacious in their pursuit of quarry were needed to fulfill such a duty.

As one of the legends goes, in searching for a dog that could meet the needs of these men, some of them tried importing the now extinct English Water Spaniel to do the required work. While possessing a great nose, it is

CANIS LUPUS

"Grandma, what big teeth you have!" The gray wolf, a familiar figure in fairy tales and legends, has had its reputation tarnished and its population pummeled over the centuries. Yet it is the descendants of this much-feared creature to which we open our homes and hearts. Our beloved dog, *Canis domesticus*, derives directly from the gray wolf, a highly social canine that lives in elaborately structured packs. In the wild, the gray wolf can range from 60 to 175 pounds, standing between 25 and 40 inches in height.

purported that this little breed had trouble with the cold water and air temperatures of the upper Midwest. This brought about the crossing of the English Water Spaniel with other more hardy breeds like the Curly-Coated Retriever and the Irish Water Spaniel, using, it is believed, smaller representatives of each of these breeds. Eventually, as the story goes, these crosses developed into the American Water Spaniel.

Another legend of the breed's roots attributes its progenitors to a cross between the Curly-Coated Retriever and the Field Spaniel. This was the belief of Dr. F. J. "Doc" Pfeifer of New London, Wisconsin, founder of the breed and a man who obtained his first AWS around 1894. The doctor claimed that every AWS he owned up to the 1930s had no likeness to the Irish Water Spaniel. It was only after the 1920s that the doctor noted cross-breedings involving the Irish and American Water Spaniel. It is this author's belief that the doctor was probably correct concerning the breed's origins, for the American Water Spaniel bears a resemblance to the Field Spaniel in size, body type and head conformation.

Also rumored to have been used in cross-breedings with the AWS is the Chesapeake Bay Retriever. It is this breed that some believed introduced the potential for an AWS to have a yellow eye color rather than the darker tone of brown often preferred by the breed's enthusiasts or the harmonizing color acceptable in the breed's standard. As some stories go, once "Chesapeake" blood was introduced to the breed it was noticed that some of the American Water Spaniels became a bit sharper and harsher of temperament and, since this was not an ideal temperament for the AWS, it would be necessary to remove or dilute the "Chesapeake" blood in the American Water Spaniel gene pool. It was believed that you could tell an AWS with "Chesapeake" blood simply by the eye color and, therefore, to remove this less desirable blood from the breed it would be best to pull any AWS with a yellow eye from the breeding pool. A remnant of that philosophy persists even to this day, as any dog found to have yellow eyes is disqualified from show competition and is considered unfit for breeding.

By most accounts the American Water Spaniel was at its peak of popularity during the late 1800s and into the early 1900s. During this time it was referred to as the American Brown Water Spaniel, the American Brown or simply the American Spaniel. As the AWS was developed for field work, it is difficult to find

accounts of the breed as a family companion in those early days, although old photographs have been found which indicate the breed was more than simply a working dog. During this time the part of the country that gave birth to the AWS was still bordering on the frontier, as one of the era's most notable authors, Laura Ingalls Wilder, recounted in her *Little House* series of children's books. These were rugged people who fought hard to make a life for

The AWS is one of the few pure-bred dogs recognized by the AKC to be developed in the US. The story is told on this Wisconsin "official marker."

their families. They did not have the luxury of owning multiple dogs, each with an assigned specialty. Theirs was a way of life that demanded that everyone pull his own weight and to do whatever job came before him. Nothing less was expected of the family dog.

Dogs of this period were expected to serve as a watchdog of sorts, warning of intruders when necessary and chasing off wayward pests, like predators looking for a quick meal from the chicken coop. The AWS and other working dogs of the time often had to be a family companion,

hunter, protector of the homestead and anything else the owner felt the dog could or should do. It is not surprising then that even today we find the AWS willing to warn of intruders on "its" property and capable of pulling double duty as both a solid flushing dog and a skilled retriever.

The American Brown of those early days was often a companion as well as a formidable hunting dog. Just a few short decades ago, it was not unusual to hear stories recanted by old-timers recalling their youth, speaking with a tear in their eye of fond memories of

The American Water Spaniel has been an integral family member since the late 1800s.

"Brownie" or "Curly" living in the house and being a devoted companion. In fact, the American Water Spaniel's friendly nature endeared it to many in those days and served to encourage people to bring the dog indoors and make it a big part of the family. Today when you come across old photographs of these early American Water Spaniels, you will probably find them poised with the rest of the family in a family photo, seated next to the mistress of the house or lying with the children, and you can see how the American Water Spaniel then, as it does today, wiggled its way into the hearts of these people. This is a testament in its own right to the power of a loving and devoted companion.

While the breed went by many names in the early years, it was finally standardized by Doc Pfeifer when he was able to obtain recognition of the breed as a pure-bred in 1920. After attempting but failing to gain recognition for the AWS by the Field Dog Stud Book and the American Kennel Club (AKC), the good doctor turned to the United Kennel Club (UKC) for acceptance of the breed's ability to replicate itself from one generation to the next. On February 8, 1920 the UKC accepted the first AWS into its registry with the admission of Curly Pfeifer into the records. Had it not been for the doctor's love of the breed he had known from childhood and his desire to see it succeed, we might not have the American Water Spaniel with us today.

Subsequent to recognition of the AWS by the UKC the breed developed a following among a number of breeders seeking to promote the breed and establish sound breeding programs. This gave rise to such notable

midwestern breeders as Driscoll Scanlan, Karl Hinz, Thomas Brogden, John Scofield and Charles Shelberg. It also brought out individuals from the Northeast, such as Louis Smith, John Sherlock and Thomas Tyler. Many of these men banded together to form the first American Water Spaniel Club (AWSC) around 1937. Through their efforts and those of many others, the AWS received recognition from the Field Dog Stud

One of the American Water Spaniel's duties in the early days, and today as well, was to keep a watchful eye over his family.

American Water Spaniels have always been considered family members and often posed for photos with their "siblings."

Book in 1938 and from the American Kennel Club in 1940.

The eventual goal of the AWSC was to obtain AKC recognition and, to that end, the men worked hard to maintain accurate records of their breeding programs, a plan that no doubt benefited from UKC recognition. Following a presentation to the AKC board of directors, the AWSC asked for recognition of the AWS as a pure-bred dog. After studying the information supplied to them, the AKC board accepted the AWS and granted recognition on May 14, 1940 and in so doing classified the AWS as a spaniel, a decision that has been and continues to be a bone of contention for some of the breed's enthusiasts.

Perhaps most unfortunate for

the AWS was the fact that its recognition by the AKC came just before the start of World War II. With the onset of the war, life throughout the United States changed, and demand for dogs declined as men left the country to go fight. Some of those breeders remaining behind maintained their kennels and continued to produce quality dogs. Some showed their dogs at AKC dog shows on a regular basis, and in 1947 a dog by the name of Happy Hiram of Ty-Grim, owned by Thomas Tyler from upstate New York, took a Group Four placement at the prestigious Westminster Kennel Club. This was the first, and to date only, Group placement of an American Water Spaniel at Westminster.

After the war the American

Whimsical photos were common around the turn of the 20th century, and the AWS was always willing to cooperate.

Water Spaniel began a steady decline in popularity, and the original AWSC disbanded, leaving the AWS without a voice in the AKC and without leadership. Men returning from the war found work in factories and began a slow exodus out of the country, moving into more urban environments. As the rural landscape and way of life changed so too did the need for sporting dogs to help put food on the table. Hunting had slowly evolved into a sport rather than a way of life or means to feed one's family, and interest in sporting dogs evolved along with it. Returning soldiers brought with them an appreciation for the dogs they had seen in Europe, and that led to an upsurge in the popularity of breeds like the German Shorthaired Pointer and specialists such as the Labrador Retriever or Pointer.

Field trials became popular among those who enjoyed sporting dogs and the sport of hunting, but these field games were limited to specific breeds of retrievers, pointers or spaniels; it seemed as though none of them had room for the AWS. Those who wished to participate in the field trials were not interested in a breed that could not participate in them, so the all-purpose AWS was left behind, but there was always a small loyal following of enthusiasts keeping it propped up and safe from extinction.

These AWS loyalists were a mixture of people with varying interests who often worked independent of one another but who occasionally shared resources. By the end of the 1940s some of the earlier breeders had grown old and were lost forever or simply could not continue to

Another AWS hamming it up for the camera with a sibling in the early days of the breed.

breed. Beginning in the 1950s and into the 1960s these breeders were replaced with the likes of Tom and Constance Rutherford, Paul Bovee and John and Marilyn Barth. Most of these breeders produced dogs not for the show ring but for what they had always

Ch. Choco Lot Morrison CDX and Ch. Little Brownie's Gunner Boy CD with owner and author Paul Morrison following a Michigan pheasant hunt.

been, a working man's hunting dog. Others did pursue the sport of show dogs and exhibited their American Water Spaniels on a fairly regular basis at AKC dog shows.

While the AWS has never set the world of dog shows on fire, many have competed and represented the breed well. From the period of the 1950s and 1960s the most popular American Water

Spaniel kennels in the dog-show world were Ty-Grim, owned by Thomas Tyler, and Americana, owned by Tom and Constance Rutherford of southeast Michigan. From the late 1960s until the mid 1980s only a handful of individuals campaigned their American Water Spaniels on a regular basis, one of the most noted being Barbara Spisak of Dayton, Ohio under the kennel name of Countrysides. Then in 1975 a group of individuals formed the American Water Spaniel Breeders Association, which only existed for a few years but laid the groundwork for another club that would eventually become today's AKC parent club for the American Water Spaniel, which encourages greater participation in the AKC world of dog shows.

The American Water Spaniel Club, Inc. was resurrected in 1985 by individuals from across the country and a number of longtime breeders like Paul Bovee, John and Marilyn Barth and Mick and Dorthea Robinson. The new AWSC, headquartered in the breed's home state of Wisconsin, quickly moved to establish itself as the voice of the American Water Spaniel in the AKC world and soon began to hold an annual dog show, obedience trials and specialized brand of hunt tests for the breed. While many contributed to the success of the AWSC, none did more than Father

Not just a hunter, Windy shows why the AWS is so valued as a companion as well.

Vaughn Brockman of Menominee, Wisconsin. Father Brockman was known as a bit of a breed historian, a successful breeder (Wildemoor kennels) and a promoter of sound breeding practices through judicious use of health screening coupled with a strict breeding regimen. A number of individuals in the new AWSC were very interested in and excited by the dog-show world and successfully campaigned American Water Spaniels throughout the Midwest and other parts of the country. Most of these individuals were associated with Father Brockman and campaigned the type of AWS that he had developed from the start of his breeding program in the early 1970s. At the time of Father Brockman's death, 20 years later, his breeding program had been so

AKC/UKC Ch.
Little Brownies
Cinnamon Teal
CDX, U-CDX,
owned by the
author Paul
Morrison.

successful and so extensive that he was credited with having created his own line of American Water Spaniels; 1 of only 3 lines generally recognized at that time and the one line most often seen in the show ring then and now.

In 1993 another club formed that was devoted to the working qualities of the American Water Spaniel. This club, the American Water Spaniel Field Association (AWSFA), was developed in an attempt to bring more focus on the working qualities of the breed and to assist owners of American

Water Spaniels with the development of their dogs as all-around field dogs. The AWSFA has focused on field training, breed rescue, the sharing of health information, training and historical aspects of the AWS, and it led the battle for field classification of the AWS with the American Kennel Club. The AWSFA is largely a regional club centered in the Great Lakes area and offering training opportunities for its members. It hopes to one day be licensed to hold AKC Spaniel Hunt Tests and AWSC Retrieving Certification Tests.

Today it is not unusual to find American Water Spaniels at dog shows around the country, but some areas are more likely to have them than others. If you are looking for a glimpse of an American Water Spaniel in the show ring, you will have the greatest luck in the upper Midwest, the Northwest and mountain states, California and certain parts of the East Coast. Today about ten or more American Water Spaniels receive AKC show championship titles in most years, a testament to the ongoing interest in the sport and the desire of AWS breeders and owners to showcase their favorite breed.

The AWS is more than a pretty face, though, and it enjoys and does well in performance events. When the sport of dog

obedience came to be in the late 1950s, AWS owners were there to showcase their little brown dogs' working abilities. Throughout most of the years since the sport became recognized by the AKC, it is possible to find the AWS participating and, in some cases, excelling at obedience. A number of American Water Spaniels have earned the Utility Dog title, one of the highest titles that can be achieved in the world of dog obedience.

With the emergence of new events like agility, flyball and rally obedience, the AWS stands poised to show its versatility to the world. Already, AWS fans have established their dogs as true competitors in the sports and made all of their fellow enthusiasts proud of their accomplishments. American Water Spaniels are successful at these sports because they possess a seemingly insatiable appetite to work in partnership with their owners. The bond that can form between an AWS and its owner is sometimes described as unbreakable, and American Water Spaniels that would otherwise excel at jobs conducted under the direction of an owner will often times flounder or absolutely refuse to perform under the direction of another person.

Of all the activities that the AWS enjoys, perhaps none is more important to it than field work. Whether you are a hunter of waterfowl or upland game, you will rarely be disappointed with the performance of the AWS. Unfortunately for the first-time buyer of an American Water Spaniel, there are few dogs that hold nationally recognized titles from any major registry, so pursuit of a pup from proven field dogs is difficult at best. Buyers must rely on the word of the breeder to assure them of the hunting ability in the parents of a puppy rather than pedigrees indicating a long lineage of ancestors who had earned numerous field titles.

The reason for this is that for decades there were only two organizations that offered nation-ally recognized hunt-test title programs for the American Water Spaniel. These organizations, the Hunting Retriever Club (HRC) and the North American Hunting Retriever Association (NAHRA), provide testing programs most suitable for the common retriever and less suited to a spaniel. This is not to say that the AWS or any other spaniel is incapable of performing the requirements of these testing programs but instead that the programs may not be as conducive to the work of the AWS and as such you may not see as many American Water Spaniels, as a percentage of the breed's population, participating in these tests as you would other breeds.

With ardent support from breeders and owners alike, American Water Spaniels can look forward to a bright future in the show ring and in the field.

Another reason for low participation in these testing programs might be the fact that many hunters who own a hunting AWS look upon them not as specialized retrievers but as all-around field dogs and as such do not feel comfortable training them for one specific task. Whatever the reason for the relatively low number of American Water Spaniels participating in the retriever hunt tests, there have still been slightly more than 20 retriever titles awarded to American Water Spaniels by these 2 organizations over the last 20 or so years. This is a good indication that with a dedicated owner and a solid training program the AWS can succeed in these hunt-test programs.

For more than 15 years there was a struggle between 3 factions of the AWS community that prevented the AWS from participating in American Kennel Club hunt tests of any type. This struggle centered on a difference of opinion over what was the more appropriate field-testing program for the American Water Spaniel available from the AKC. The AKC requires a sporting breed's parent club to declare the type of test that the breed will be allowed to participate in, and the members of the AWSC could not come to an agreement on which program was best. Therefore, for well over a decade the breed was unable to participate in any AKC

field-testing program. Then in 2004 a compromise resolution was brought before the membership of the AWSC.

This resolution called upon the membership to accept AKC field classification of the AWS as a flushing spaniel, allowing it to participate in AKC Spaniel Hunt Tests and requiring that the breed also pass a special Retrieving Certificate Test designed, monitored and awarded by the AWSC. The resolution was passed by a large majority of AWSC members and was accepted by the AKC board of directors in November of 2004. As a result of this compromise agreement, the AWS was able to begin participating in AKC hunt tests as of June 1, 2005. It became just the second AKC-recognized sporting breed that must meet both the AKC requirements for an AKC hunt-test title and the parent club's requirement for a special certificate before any AKC field title can be awarded. The reason this action was taken was to assure those concerned that the AKC hunt-test program would not adversely impact the American Water Spaniel's historical working qualities and that steps were being taken to prevent a disintegration of the breed's field abilities. By combining the upland work of AKC Spaniel Hunt Tests with the water-retrieving work of the AWSC Retrieving Certificate

Test, it is believed that the field qualities of the AWS will remain solidly intact and help to assure the preservation of the breed as an all-around hunting companion.

Preserving the American Water Spaniel is a concern of many of the breed's enthusiasts. As of the end of 2005 the AWS ranked 128 out of 154 breeds recognized by the American Kennel Club with just 187 dogs registered, and it was the fifth least popular sporting breed recognized by the American Kennel Club. This low number of registrations and dubious distinction reflect a continuing trend for the AWS. Whether or not this trend can be reversed and the number of AWS registrations returned to its higher levels of 15 years earlier is yet to be seen. One thing is for certain, those who choose to bring an AWS into their lives are rewarded with the love of a curly-haired, brown dog

Today's American Water Spaniel still retains the water instincts that he acquired from his early ancestors.

whose personality, tenacity and spirit will fill their lives with great joy for years to come.

In testament to the enduring qualities of the American Water Spaniel are two stories of recognition and honor bestowed upon the breed. The first took place in Arizona during the 1930s, and it landed one AWS by the name of "Johnnie" some national publicity when he appeared in a cartoon by Robert Ripley as part of his *Ripley's Believe It or Not!* series. Johnnie was owned by Dixie Lee Brayton, the daughter of Arizona Representative Nelson D. Brayton from Miami, Arizona. Apparently Johnnie often visited the capitol building when the legislature was in session and roamed the halls of the "chambers checking up on the membership, occasionally stopping at the press table to growl." At some point the then Speaker of the House, Vernon G. Davis, decided that Johnnie could not be wandering through the capitol without official approval and issued the AWS a card which read: "Arizona House of Representatives, Thirteenth Legislature, Phoenix, Arizona, Feb. 5, 1937, Johnnie (House Mascot) (of) Miami, Arizona, is entitled to entrance to house on official business. Approved, Signed, Vernon G. Davis, Speaker of the House."

Besides being the official Arizona state house mascot,

Johnnie was also known for sneaking away from home and going down to the local football field to watch his buddies playing football. Once there he would wait for the opportunity to run out and snatch up the football so that he could show the players some real moves. One of his most famous exploits in this regard was in 1931 when he grabbed the ball off the field during the annual game between the Globe and Miami teams. He picked up the ball in his mouth between downs and ran all the way downfield for a touchdown that was subsequently denied by the referee. Johnnie was probably quite upset about that ruling, but it did not deter him from continuing to play the game of football whenever the opportunity arose.

A more recent honor was bestowed not upon one specific AWS but on the entire breed by the state of Wisconsin when it designated the American Water Spaniel as its official state dog. The effort to obtain such recognition had been driven over a number of years by the students of the eighth grade social studies classes at Washington Middle School in New London, Wisconsin, home to the breed's founder Dr. F. J. Pfeifer. Their teacher, Lyle Brumm, had come up with the idea of teaching the children a bit about the legislative process through an actual project

Max, owned by Aaron Glann, displays one of his first ducks.

to lobby for the passage of a bill designating the AWS as the state dog. Over a period of five years, these middle-school students worked tirelessly to obtain the designation. Through their efforts and those of a few other notable Wisconsin personalities, the bill passed and became law on April 22, 1986, when then Governor Anthony Earl signed the bill, making the American Water Spaniel just one of a few breeds honored as a state dog.

THE AWS IN EUROPE
In recent years the American Water Spaniel has made its way beyond the confines of the US and is beginning to strike the fancy of a few Europeans. In 1995 the first of a series of exports to the Czech Republic took place and formed

The author Paul
Morrison and his
wife Lynn pose
for a family
portrait with
their "children."

The author Paul Morrison and his wife Lynn pose for a family portrait with their "children."

the foundation stock for a breeding program that is now nearly ten years old. All in all, two Czech breeders, Jiri Fiala and Josef Sos, imported seven American Water Spaniels from a variety of kennels in an effort to maintain genetic diversity. These breeders have successfully produced pups that have performed well in field tests and conformation shows held in central and western Europe.

In 2005 two individuals from Finland imported American Water Spaniels as potential breeding stock. For Maria Miettinen of Helsinki, Finland, this was her second AWS after having obtained another dog seven years earlier. Maria's first dog, Misty, was obtained chiefly as a pet but was so well received at dog shows and performance events that it gave Maria some added incentive to increase the population of American Water Spaniels in Finland by at least one. An acquaintance of hers, Tiina Narhi, was also intrigued by the breed and decided to see how an AWS might work out in her home. Recently both dogs were reportedly doing quite well, having won honors at local dog shows and having demonstrated their love of field work. It looks like the AWS is off to a fine start in Finland.

Great Britain also saw the importation of a couple of American Water Spaniels in 2004. Gina Bowers, who hails from England, visited with a breeder in southern California while on a trip to the area. There she fell in love with the breed and obtained her first AWS. She also saw a couple of American Water Spaniels being exhibited at a dog show in Hungary that belonged to the breeders in the Czech Republic and chose to import a dog from there to be a companion to Raz, Gina's first AWS. Because England's Kennel Club does not yet recognize the American Water Spaniel, Gina is working hard to introduce the breed to the country and to gain Kennel Club recognition. There is little doubt in the minds of most AWS owners that the American Water Spaniel will win the hearts and favor of many in Britain, just as it has done in other parts of Europe and in North America.

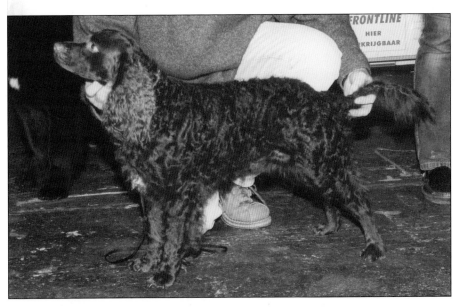

Night Hawks Sweet Chocolate "stacked" and ready for a conformation show.

CHARACTERISTICS OF THE

AMERICAN WATER SPANIEL

GENERAL CHARACTERISTICS

The American Water Spaniel is a friendly and outgoing dog interested in being near the action and often times wanting to take center stage. Seldom do you meet up with an aloof AWS who seemingly wants nothing to do with you. The visitor to an American Water Spaniel's home will often find the dog begging for a petting, offering up a ball for a game of fetch or snuggling into a comfortable place in the visitor's lap. For most dog lovers this is a minor inconvenience, and for many others it is a welcome reception. Still owners should understand that such behavior is not always welcome by guests and take steps to teach the dog to come under more acceptable control when required.

American Water Spaniels are often described as intelligent dogs that take to training well. The breed loves attention and is very willing to please its trainer. Because of this it often trains quickly, leading many newcomers to the breed to cease to continue with the training after the dog has picked up on the basic commands; this is where trouble can begin. Without continued training, an AWS will begin to be obedient enough to avoid getting himself into too much trouble but not obedient enough to be the pleasant companion he can be. When this happens some will describe the dog as manipulative or cunning. In reality the dog has simply learned that by exhibiting specific behaviors at the short-term expense of others, he is able to get his way most of the time. Diligent owners who regularly

Not only a force to be reckoned with in the field, the American Water Spaniel is second to none as a loyal companion as well.

train and socialize their dogs through early adulthood will find that they can avoid this type of behavior.

People searching for a new companion often raise the question of just how compatible the breed is with children, strangers and other dogs. While there are exceptions to the rule, most American Water Spaniels do well with all of these. When it comes to children it is always best to err on the side of caution. The wise owner will be very watchful of the interaction between the dog and children, especially children under five years of age. The fast moves and loud play of young children are sometimes stressful to dogs, and such stress can result in negative canine behaviors. Parents need to understand that it is as necessary to train their children in the proper way to behave around the dog as it is to train the dog in how to act with children.

A dog that demonstrates a dislike of strange people and other dogs is sometimes nothing more than a dog that was not properly socialized during early puppyhood. Of course this is not always the case, and some dogs are simply born with an aversion to strangers of all types. Luckily with the AWS this is not normally the case. To help assure that a more pleasant personality is brought out in the AWS puppy,

HEART-HEALTHY
In this modern age of ever-improving cardio-care, no doctor or scientist can dispute the advantages of owning a dog to lower a person's risk of heart disease. Studies have proven that petting a dog, walking a dog and grooming a dog all show positive results toward lowering your blood pressure. The simple routine of exercising your dog—going outside with the dog and walking, jogging or playing catch—is heart-healthy in and of itself. If you are normally less active than your physician thinks you should be, adopting a dog may be a smart option to improve your own quality of life as well as that of another creature.

Neither rain, nor sleet nor snow can keep the versatile American Water Spaniel down. This AWS is ready for whatever Mother Nature throws at him.

within the social hierarchy of the household and will attempt to move up the pecking order if given the opportunity. As this occurs owners may see signs of the breed's possessiveness as their AWS growls or quickly grabs an object when the owner reaches for it. When this happens the dog is saying, "This is mine and you cannot have it" and illustrating his possessive tendency. A thorough training and socialization program can help to minimize or even prevent this type of behavior from ever developing. If such behavior should occur, it is often correctable with the use of a regimented retraining program supervised by a qualified trainer.

If there is one single annoying behavior to be found in the American Water Spaniel, it is its propensity to bark. This is a vocal breed that seemingly loves to hear itself and will even "give tongue" when chasing rabbits in the field or other dogs in play. The slightest noise or movement can set off a series of barks so incessant that it will drive even the most patient of individuals crazy. American Water Spaniels have been known to go into a prolonged barking frenzy over things like songbirds feeding in the back yard, squirrels foraging for nuts or a shoe dropped on the floor. Training will help this problem, but it is one that will

new owners should attend puppy socialization classes and take steps to introduce their dogs to new experiences throughout their formative years.

The American Water Spaniel is often described as possessive and protective. These traits bear some relationship to one another and are sometimes reflective of the dog's understanding of its rank within the family unit or pack. The breed has a tendency to occasionally challenge its rank stay with many for their entire life. For this reason many breeders do not recommend the breed as one for apartment living unless steps can be taken to minimize or eliminate the dog's inclination to bark.

While immensely enjoying its own vocalizations may not sound like an endearing quality, some American Water Spaniels do have the ability to turn this sometimes annoying characteristic into a rather charmingly attractive occurrence. Those are the dogs that are blessed with the ability and propensity to yodel. While the sound emitted by a yodeling AWS is more like a howl than what one might recognize as a true yodel, it does fall a little short of the annoying howls we often attribute to other canines. Oftentimes the yodel seems to be roused by happiness or excitement, such as during play, at feeding time or when guests arrive for a visit. One of my first American Water Spaniels was a champion yodeler who loved to hear himself so much that I was able to teach him to respond to the command to yodel with good reliability. Not all American Water Spaniels bear this trait, but once found within a household, it is one that is sorely missed should it ever fall silent.

When it comes to housing, this is not a breed that does well living in a pen, fenced-in yard or chained to a tree all day, every day. Because the AWS enjoys, and in some cases demands, human contact, these dogs should not be left alone for long periods of time. Such abandonment will lead to excessive barking, lack of social skills and unwanted behaviors like digging or fence climbing. The AWS should be a member of the family brought into the household, loved and cared for just like any other family member. When this is done, and the proper steps are taken to train and socialize the dog, it will be a canine companion like few others.

American Water Spaniels are active dogs that do best when given a job to do and some good physical exercise. While they do not need long periods of exercise it is best to give them the opportunity to run off some of their sporting energy regularly. Of

The activity level of a sporting breed is normally quite high, and the American Water Spaniel is no exception; this AWS can hardly contain himself, waiting to get back into the water.

California Chocolate Chip, better known as "Callie," demonstrating the AWS's capacity for retrieval.

"Well, are you coming or what?" The AWS must be given plenty of exercise and duties to remain a delightful companion.

course, a good 20- or 30-minute walk each morning and night will serve to keep them in the best physical and mental condition but so too will a nice romp in the back yard each day or a few play dates at the local park each week. An idle AWS will become overweight and bored, leading to both health and behavior

problems like excessive chewing or barking. If you have an American Water Spaniel, take the time to enjoy his company by playing fetch in the back yard or learning a sport like hunting, agility or competitive obedience so both of you will be rewarded with a long and healthy relationship.

Some AWS owners will tell you that the breed is a "garbage can," willing to devour anything and everything that enters its mouth. Stories have been told of American Water Spaniels who have eaten various articles of clothing, tennis balls, golf balls, rubber door stops, plastic plates and much more. The breed will seemingly search out and locate the vilest items around the field or yard and promptly make a feast of them. Therefore it is best to train a puppy as to what is a proper chew toy or food item and to teach him the "Leave it" command for when you want something left alone or immediately dropped, if the dog already has it in his mouth.

There have been some breeders and individuals who claim the American Water Spaniel is "hypoallergenic," making it a safe breed for allergy sufferers to bring into their home. Unfortunately this is not truly the case. The breed sheds hair and produces dander, both of which can be a catalyst to allergic reactions. Despite anecdotal claims that people with allergies are less sensitive to the AWS than to other breeds, it is not recommended that allergy sufferers, especially those with severe allergies, introduce an AWS into their home.

The AWS is probably best described as a moderately shedding dog that constantly loses coat. Most owners do not see the shedding as a nuisance except, perhaps, for the one time each year when many of the dogs will shed their winter coats over a period of a few weeks, leaving behind enough hair to outfit another dog. The coat texture of an AWS is normally fine rather than coarse, and the shed hair does not have a tendency to embed itself into the carpet or other fabric the way the coat of other breeds can. The few problems that do come from shedding can be partially alleviated by regular brushing and bathing when necessary.

Alex Glam Streeter or "Mad Max" proudly poses for the camera with his hunter.

IN THE FIELD

The American Water Spaniel has always been an all-around hunting dog and, with luck and support, will remain one for many years to come. As a hunting dog it possesses sufficient energy to work the fields and woodlands for all types of game, ranging from pheasants to grouse and even the occasional rabbit. While it holds an energy level that allows it to go all day in the field, it also maintains the willingness to sit patiently in the blind waiting for the next flight of ducks or geese to swoop in to the decoys. Patience is not a virtue that comes without training, however, and it is the wise owner who begins this training at an early age.

As a retriever the American Water Spaniel is best suited to work marshes, rivers, small lakes and the like for waterfowl. While more than a few American Water Spaniels have been used to retrieve from the big waters of the Great Lakes and along the ocean shorelines, when a sudden storm develops such water can quickly become too much of a challenge for this medium-sized breed.

The breed is good at marking the location of fallen game, and it will normally do so quickly and with great enthusiasm. It is not unusual to hear hunters tell stories of six or eight birds falling from the sky and their American Water Spaniels sitting patiently, waiting for the command to retrieve. Once sent on the retrieve the dog often successfully gathers each and every bird without further direction from the owner. Despite such stories, though, it is the wise owner who takes the time to thoroughly train the AWS in the proper field manners of retrieving dogs. Teaching the dog to sit quietly as it waits to be sent on its task and instructing it on how to be directed to a downed bird are just a couple of the trained behaviors most owners should work on. Through judicious and consistent training, owners will find that the AWS will perform in the stylized fashion of many of the common retriever breeds.

When hunting the uplands for pheasants, grouse or rabbit, the AWS makes good use of its exceptional nose. It is not unusual to hear owners brag of their dogs scenting birds well out of gun range. Similarly, it is quite common to hear stories of dogs that tracked wounded game for several yards and then dug it out of cover so dense that the hunter could not see the dog once it entered the cover. Such is the power of the AWS's nose and the tenacity of the breed's spirit.

Historically, the need for a medium-sized field dog that wouldn't "tip the boat" on a hunt gave rise to the development of the AWS.

Though a flushing breed, the AWS is not what some would describe as a hard-flushing dog. Instead the American Water Spaniel tends to put a bird to flight with more of a soft flush as it moves into the bird judiciously as opposed to recklessly. Once the bird is put to flight the AWS will chase after it unless taught the proper manners of being steady to the flush of the bird or at least heeding the command of its owner to sit.

Field training should begin at an early age with basic obedience and simple retrieves. This is not the time to overdo the work expected of the dog, so short sessions of no more than a 10- or 15-minute duration held 2 or 3 times each day will quickly form a solid basis on which to develop a good working dog. As training progresses the introduction of birds, guns, gunfire, decoys and other typical aspects found while hunting can begin. It is very important that all of these things be introduced in a systematic and positive manner so as to encourage the dog to develop its inherent qualities as a field dog.

For the novice trainer there are many books available to help in getting started with the training process. It is often best to avail yourself of a couple of books to develop an understanding of the various techniques used and to find a program that best fits your needs and personality. There are

The American Water Spaniel's webbed feet and all-around field abilities make it a natural and confident water retriever.

also numerous training clubs and professional trainers around the country that will assist members in accomplishing the task of creating a good flushing dog or retriever, and new owners will benefit from searching out such groups to assist them with the process. What is most important is that the novice trainer seeks assistance so that the training techniques used are appropriate and will lead to success for both the dog and trainer.

SPANIEL OR RETRIEVER
If you find yourself among a number of American Water Spaniel owners and want to effect a strong debate, just ask the question, "Are these spaniels or retrievers?" The answer will vary from owner to owner and probably be centered more upon how each owner uses his dog in

the field than on the actual characteristics of the breed.

This has been a long-standing debate among AWS field enthusiasts and is likely the root cause for the delay in classifying the breed with the American Kennel Club. Even the solution to ending the debate over classification involved a compromise of sorts that permitted the two sides of the argument to meet somewhat in the middle with the spaniel supporters gaining AKC classification as a flushing spaniel and the retriever supporters obtaining a requirement that no title is awarded until a dog demonstrates its ability as a retriever in American Water Spaniel Club Retrieving Certificate Tests.

It has long been stated that the chief cause for the debate about "spaniel or retriever" is found in the breed's name, the American Water Spaniel. If it were not for throwing that word "water" into the name there might never have been this controversy and people may have been more accepting of the breed's abilities as an all-around hunting dog. It may also have been helpful if there would have been a designation by the American Kennel Club or some other voice of authority defining just what a water spaniel is and what it does so that it could be compared to other types of dogs like

Tangle, owned by Jim McKibben, with one of several ducks retrieved during a morning's hunt in Wisconsin.

retrievers, pointers or spaniels.

While the answer to this debate may never be determined, one can look to noted experts to find a clue to the likely answer that may actually lay this matter to rest. First is to find a definition of just what a water spaniel is, and we get somewhat of an explanation from John R. Falk's *The Complete Guide To Bird Dog Training*, where he describes the American Water Spaniel as a dog that was "...developed principally for duck hunting, his versatility was recognized early on and even in the latter part of the nineteenth century he saw considerable work springing marsh birds in the lowlands and ruffed grouse and rabbits in the uplands." It is this versatility to function both as a retriever and as a flushing dog along the varied cover of wetland areas that makes a water spaniel.

So, according to Falk, we should not look upon a water spaniel as simply a retriever but as much more. It should be a versatile dog that is capable of flushing game and retrieving it from land or water. This is in keeping with the writings of many of the breed's early developers and supporters, including Driscoll Scanlan, who was quoted by Howard Peterson in 1938 as saying, "As a retriever the American water spaniel is well-nigh perfect by nature...The American water spaniel is equally at home afield or astream.

Endowed with a faultless nose, this breed works thicket, rough ground or almost impenetrable covert, depending on body scent for game location...It does not point game but springs it...The dogs are easily trained, quick to learn to drop to wing and shot."

If that is not enough to help settle the debate one can also read the words of John Scofield, a prominent breeder of the 1940s and 1950s who wrote, "There seems even today some confusion on the part of individuals who want to classify the American as a Retriever. This is a mistake and should never be considered. The American is typical Spaniel; his heritage proves that beyond a doubt, and the American Kennel Club upholds that Spaniel classi-fication."

Looking back at the writings of the breed's originators and early promoters helps us to see exactly how they looked upon the AWS and its special fit in the world of sporting dogs. With the advent of American Kennel Club classifica-tions and the special testing program established by the AWSC, maintaining the American Water Spaniel as more than simply a retriever should be easier. With AWS owners able to test the versatility of the breed rather than relegating it to nothing more than retriever tests, the breed should stay true to its root heritage and characteristics.

AMERICAN WATER SPANIEL

For 50 years, from the time of initial AKC recognition, the American Water Spaniel's breed standard remained unchanged. Then, in 1990, at the urging of the AKC and in an attempt to better explain key aspects of the breed's physical characteristics, the standard was changed to that which is found today. The standard is used as a blueprint for the breed's ideal physical structure and serves as a guide breeders should follow when choosing to produce quality American Water Spaniels. The breed standard also serves as a measure by which judges can evaluate dogs presented to them at conformation shows. By seeking out the opinion of conformation judges and evaluating one dog against others of its kind, breeders are able to make more informed decisions regarding the dogs best suited for their particular breeding program.

Most American Water Spaniel breeders understand that maintaining the breed's physical characteristics is as important as maintaining the breed's original purpose as an all-around hunting dog. People choosing to breed their American Water Spaniels should pay particular attention to the symmetry of the

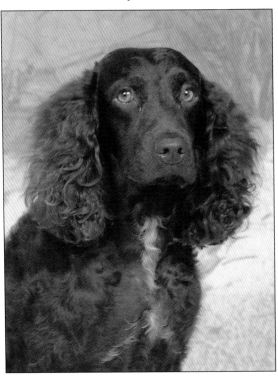

A little white on the chest or toes of the American Water Spaniel is permissible by the AKC breed standard.

breed's physical qualities and to avoid overdoing one characteristic for another. Novices will do well to seek the advice of a knowledgeable AWS breeder and to work with the person from whom they obtained their AWS, if that person has himself been breeding for a substantial period of time. Such breeders will have the best understanding of the strengths and weaknesses found within their own line of dogs and thus can best direct the novice along a positive path.

One of the first physical

This is a fine example of a marcel-coated American Water Spaniel.

attention-grabbing characteristics of the AWS is the breed's coat. The coat can be curly, marcel or some variation of the two. What the coat should not be is straight or flat, except in specific areas of the body which include the face, forehead and fronts of the legs. A dog whose coat is predominately flat does not properly represent the American Water Spaniel's ideal coat type. The term marcel is used to describe a wavy coat pattern as opposed to one that is curly and is a term that is often misunderstood by newcomers to the breed. Such individuals should remember that the breed was first recognized in the 1920s, an era that produced "speakeasies" and female dancers called "flappers." It was one of the flapper hairstyles that was worn tight to the skin with uniform waves that most likely influenced the term

Dogs in the show ring are not compared against each other but rather against the breed standard. The dog that most closely conforms to the breed standard, in the judge's opinion, is the winner of the class.

used to describe a wavy-coated American Water Spaniel as marcel.

An American Water Spaniel's coat should be sufficiently dense so as to protect against cold temperatures, and it should shed water quickly. The texture of the coat should be soft rather than coarse, and it should not be brittle. The coat should appear healthy and not dull. The body should be well covered with hair, and the coat should be moderate in length. Unfortunately there is no definition of what constitutes a moderate length of coat, so you may see coats with hair that is no more than an inch or two in length and others that are much longer. This is especially the case with

the feathering on the legs and tail.

Some American Water Spaniels have excessively long feathering which is more like that of a setter than of a spaniel, but because there is not a specific definition of the term "moderate," all are taken to be acceptable even though this is probably not truly the case.

In reading some literature from the early days of recognition, it is obvious that the full coats often seen in the show ring today were not those intended by at least some of the breed's early promoters. In fact, the standard prior to 1990 called for a tail that was covered to the tip, which could be covered by curls, feathering or some combination of the two, while today's standard requires a tail that is feathered.

Of course you cannot look upon an American Water Spaniel without being drawn to its rich brown color. The AWS is always a shade of brown ranging from liver to brown to chocolate. This too is a departure from the breed's original standard which called for the dogs to be either liver or dark chocolate. Today you will not find a dog registered after 1990 that carries the designation of dark chocolate, yet it is obvious that this was one of the original color variations of the breed. While the liver color is typically considered to be a shade of brown having a deep red tone, the chocolate is more of a dark brown resembling the color of a dark chocolate candy bar. Noticeably absent in the AWS is any form of marking or ticking except for the occasional white which can be found on the chest or feet. White should be kept to a minimum, as the standard calls for "a little white" and lists it as permissible. How much white constitutes a "little" is left up to the particular individual to decide, but certainly the white should not be so extensive as to draw the eye from other qualities of the dog. While white on the chest is not at all rare, the author has only seen one adult American Water Spaniel with white on a toe.

In order for a dog to be a top performer in the field, it must have the ability to move well and be agile enough to respond to changes in the terrain. For this to happen you need a dog that is well muscled, balanced and relatively free of abnormal structure. Dogs that are cow-hocked, bull-legged or otherwise poorly structured may make fine

pets, but they will be hindered in their field performance by reduced agility, stamina and longevity of life. Breeders should pay particular attention to such structure and strive to reduce the occurrence of such problems. A balanced dog is one that moves freely and symmetrically, with seemingly little to no effort. A properly proportioned and structured AWS, as called for in the breed's standard, will be such a dog.

Remembering the purpose for which the breed was developed should be at the forefront of breeding decisions and striving to produce a dog that is "solidly built and well-muscled" will help to assure

Head study in profile showing correct type, structure and proportion.

that the breed can maintain the "strength and quality" necessary to continue functioning as a good all-around field dog. What individuals should seek to avoid is overdoing any one characteristic of the breed which could impair the dog rather than improve upon it. Often dogs bred more to accentuate qualities that set them apart in the show ring are dogs that lack the finer qualities of a field dog. Following the blueprint laid out by the breed standard should help anyone who chooses to breed the American Water Spaniel, maintaining that delicate balance between form and function.

Friendliness and an eagerness to please are required by the breed standard. This AWS has both and then some.

THE AMERICAN KENNEL CLUB STANDARD FOR THE AMERICAN WATER SPANIEL

General Appearance
The American Water Spaniel was developed in the United States as an all-around hunting dog, bred to retrieve from skiff or canoes and work ground with relative ease. The American Water Spaniel is an active muscular dog, medium in size with a marcel to curly coat. Emphasis is placed on proper size and a symmetrical relationship of parts, texture of coat and color.

Size, Proportion, Substance
15 to 18 inches for either sex. Males weighing 30–45 lbs. Females weighing 25–40 lbs. Females tend to be slightly smaller than the males. There is no preference for size within the given range of either sex providing correct proportion, good substance and balance is maintained. *Proportion*—is slightly longer than tall, not too square or compact. However, exact proportion is not as important as the dog being well-balanced and sound, capable of performing the breed's intended function. *Substance*—a solidly built and well-muscled dog full of strength and quality. The breed has as much substance and bone as necessary to carry the muscular structure but not so much as to appear clumsy.

Dog in profile showing correct type, structure, and proportion and correct mature coat.

Head

The head must be in proportion to the overall dog. Moderate in length. *Expression*—is alert, self-confident, attractive and intelligent. Medium size *eyes* set well apart, while slightly rounded, should not appear protruding or bulging. Lids tight, not drooping. Eye color can range from a light yellowish brown to brown, hazel or of dark tone to harmonize with coat. Disqualify yellow eyes. Yellow eyes are a bright color like that of lemon, not to be confused with the light yellowish brown. *Ears* set slightly above the eye line but not too high on the head, lobular, long and wide with leather extending to nose. *Skull* rather broad and full, stop moderately defined, but not too pronounced. *Muzzle* moderate in length, square with good depth. No inclination to snipiness. The lips are clean and tight without excess skin or flews. *Nose* dark in color, black or dark brown. The nose sufficiently wide and with well-developed nostrils to insure good scenting power. *Bite* either scissors or level.

Neck, Topline, Body

Neck round and of medium length, strong and muscular, free of throatiness, set to carry head with dignity, but arch not accentuated. *Topline* level or

FAULTS IN PROFILE

Thin ewe-necked, long back, high in the rear, weak in the pasterns, flat feet, weak rear, snipey muzzle, too fine-boned.

Generally too heavy and coarse, head and muzzle coarse, short thick neck, upright shoulders, soft topline, high in the rear, lacking angulation behind.

of the back. The tail is tapered, lively and covered with hair with moderate feathering.

Forequarters
Shoulders sloping, clean and muscular. Legs medium in length, straight and well-boned but not so short as to handicap for field work or so heavy as to appear clumsy. Pasterns strong with no suggestion of weakness. Toes closely grouped, webbed and well-padded. Size of feet to harmonize with size of dog. Front dewclaws are permissible.

Hindquarters
Well-developed hips and thighs with the whole rear assembly showing strength and drive. The hock joint slightly rounded, should not be small and sharp in contour, moderately angulated. Legs from hock joint to foot pad moderate in length, strong and straight with good bone structure. Hocks parallel.

Coat
Coat can range from marcel (uniform waves) to closely curled. The amount of waves or curls can vary from one area to another on the dog. It is important to have undercoat to provide sufficient

slight, straight slope from withers. *Body* well-developed, sturdily constructed but not too compactly coupled. Well-developed brisket extending to elbow neither too broad nor too narrow. The ribs well-sprung, but not so well-sprung that they interfere with the movement of the front assembly. The loins strong, but not having a tucked-up look. *Tail* is moderate in length, curved in a rocker fashion, can be carried either slightly below or above the level density to be of protection against weather, water or punishing cover, yet not too coarse or too soft. The throat, neck and rear of the dog well-covered with hair. The ear well-covered with hair on both sides with ear canal evident upon inspection. Forehead covered with short smooth hair and without topknot. Tail covered with hair to tip with moderate feathering. Legs have moderate feathering with waves or curls to harmonize with coat of dog. Coat may be trimmed to present a well groomed appearance; the ears may be shaved; but neither is required.

Color
Color either solid liver, brown or dark chocolate. A little white on toes and chest permissible.

Gait
The American Water Spaniel moves with well-balanced reach and drive. Watching a dog move toward one, there should be no signs of elbows being out. Upon viewing the dog from the rear, one should get the impression that the hind legs, which should be well-muscled and not cowhocked, move as nearly parallel as possible, with hocks doing their full share of work and flexing well,

thus giving the appearance of power and strength.

Temperament
Demeanor indicates intelligence, eagerness to please and friendly. Great energy and eagerness for the hunt yet controllable in the field.

Disqualification
Yellow eyes.

**Approved March 13, 1990
Effective May 1, 1990**

FAULTS IN PROFILE

Domed topskull, upright loaded shoulders, toes out in front, low on leg, soft topline, tail carried too high, lacking angulation behind.

Upright shoulders, toes in front, steep in the croup, kinked tail, weak rear and cow-hocked.

AMERICAN WATER SPANIEL

FINDING AND CHOOSING AN AMERICAN WATER SPANIEL PUPPY

FINDING A BREEDER

If you have decided that the American Water Spaniel is the breed for you, it is now time to begin searching for a breeder. Because of the rarity of this breed it is unlikely that you will find one sitting in a local pet store, waiting for some caring soul to take it home; however, if you do, proceed with caution. Such dogs have likely come from a rather questionable breeder who has failed to provide the pup with the needed social interaction so well recognized as essential to a dog's emotional

The healthiest pups come from the healthiest parents. A reputable breeder provides the best care for all of his dogs and only breeds from those who are tested as free of hereditary problems.

health. Another place to avoid locating a breeder is by searching your local newspaper listings. Again, the rarity of this breed usually makes such listings few and far between, but a breeder who advertises in this manner is likely to be someone who simply happened to have a female that he decided to breed to a local stud dog for some reason and not necessarily in an effort to improve upon the breed. Puppies from such breedings may bring you years of heartache or years of great joy, but it is a much larger gamble to get your puppy here rather than from a reputable and established breeder.

The first resource to approach for finding a reputable breeder is any club devoted to the American Water Spaniel. You can locate such clubs by contacting the American Kennel Club, which sometimes also has a listing of breeders advertising on either their website or in their magazine, the *AKC Gazette*. Clubs can usually be found through searches conducted on the Internet and will often provide a list of breeders that can be printed from their site or obtained by writing the club's secretary. Because clubs

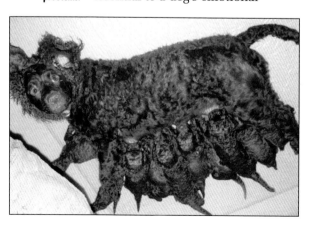

usually have a breeder's code of ethics that all of their listed breeders are encouraged to follow, you can expect to be dealing with a reputable breeder when talking to and perhaps purchasing a pup from such individuals. Further, most breeders, located in this manner, are often aware of lesser known or new breeders that they can refer you to who may be able to provide you with a pup as well. You can usually be confident that if such a breeder is recommending a lesser known or inexperienced person, that individual is someone they trust to be raising the puppies responsibly.

Finally, one of the most common ways to locate a breeder today is through the Internet. A simple search for "American Water Spaniel breeders" will return a plethora of contact sites, including

club websites, breeder-referral lists and breeder's individual websites with contact phone numbers, email and postal addresses.

SELECTING A BREEDER
So, what is a reputable breeder? While there is some variance in determining just what constitutes a

A good breeder has the best interest of the breed in mind and can dedicate the time and care to raising the pups right.

Your AWS puppy comes to you as a blank canvas; it is up to you to turn him into a work of art through proper care, training and love.

If the breeder has children at home, this is very good socialization for the puppy and will benefit anyone looking to get a puppy from that breeder.

reputable breeder, it can be said that such a breeder:

- Screens the puppy's dam and sire for common health problems such as hip dysplasia, genetic eye disorders, hypothyroidism and cardiac abnormalities
- Provides appropriate prenatal care to the dam and uses the services of a qualified veterinarian to watch over the health of the pups
- Raises the puppies in a home environment rather than in a barn, outside kennel or garage
- Interacts with the pups throughout the time they live with the breeder and exposes them to common life experiences to avoid social problems in the future
- Feeds a quality dog food to both the dam and the pups appropriate to their needs
- Assures that the pups are wormed, at least two times, and has, at a minimum, their first set of vaccines administered prior to going to their new homes

- Provides a permanent form of identification such as a tattoo or microchip for each pup before it leaves the breeder's care
- Provides a written health guarantee covering a minimum of genetically based health disorders
- Supplies American Kennel Club registration papers with each puppy sold.

As both a buyer and a breeder the author believes that it is best to call rather than write the breeder and discuss your interest in the breed. Now is the time to ask the hard questions. Go through the list of items that make for a reputable breeder to see how closely this person complies with it. Tell the breeder just why you have decided on an American Water Spaniel and ask if your reasoning seems appropriate to him. Explain a bit about your lifestyle, your home environment and your experience with dogs to give the breeder an idea of the type of temperament that would best suit your needs. Then ask if the breeder feels that the pups he normally produces would be a good match with your future plans.

If your conversation goes well and you are comfortable with the breeder, ask if he is comfortable with you. If so, then you may have found the appropriate person from whom to obtain a puppy. It is now time to discuss the cost of the pup and how long you will have to wait before a puppy will be available; it is not unusual to wait for as much as nine months or more for an available puppy. If everything still seems like a good fit for you then it is probably time to either send a deposit in for a puppy or to be put on a waiting list for the next litter.

SELECTING A PUPPY
A good breeder will usually not let the pups go to their homes prior to the age of eight weeks, and it is not uncommon for some to wait until they are ten or more weeks of age. Most American Water Spaniel breeders will encourage you to visit the litter so that you can see the dam and, hopefully, the sire prior to picking up your puppy. This allows you to get an idea of the temperament of the dam and the pups by observing their interaction with each other and yourself. It also provides you with an opportunity to see the cleanliness of the home environment, to observe the care which is administered to the pups and the dam and to find any illness that may be evident in the pups. For this reason, it is best to visit the puppies at least one time prior to picking up your puppy or making a decision on which puppy to take home.

Truth be told, most American Water Spaniel breeders do not allow you to pick your own puppy and even when they do, most buyers do not live close enough to a breeder to do so. Do not look upon this as a bad situation, for it is more appropriate for the breeder to choose the puppy best suited to your wants and needs than it is for you to do so. Why? Simple, the reputable breeder has lived with the pups night and day for eight weeks. He has gotten to know each one as an individual and has come to understand the personality that has emerged in the pup. If you have been honest with him about your expectations and lifestyle, there is no better person to choose the best pup for you than the breeder himself. Of course, this means that you have to put your full faith and

A young AWS should appear bright, alert and inquisitive.

Puppies that grow up with children form a special bond with their human "siblings."

A happy and healthy mom usually means happy and healthy pups.

trust in the breeder, and if you are not willing to do that, then you should not be dealing with that breeder to begin with. Even when you live close enough to a breeder to pick up or pick out your own puppy, most American Water Spaniel breeders will still choose the puppy that will be going home with you.

For those buyers who are given the opportunity to choose their own pup, though, here are some things to consider. The first place to begin is by examining the pups for signs of poor health before deciding to take one home. Excessively runny eyes or noses may be a sign of illness. Pale gums and diarrhea are definite signs of a problem and should be addressed with the breeder. If you are in doubt about the puppies' health then err on the side of caution. Tell the breeder of your concern and ask to pick your pup at a later date when the pups appear to be

healthy. If the breeder is unwilling to do this then run, don't walk, away and find another breeder.

After establishing that the pups are healthy and well cared for, you will now turn to observing their temperament. At this point it is good to remember that what you see at six, eight or ten weeks of age is not necessarily what you will get in an adult dog. Therefore, the temperament visible to you the day you pick out your pup is only indicative of the pup's temperament that day and not likely to be the dog's temperament as an adult. You should expect any pup, like any child, to go through various stages of development prior to reaching maturity. In the end, what you get will be a dog whose temperament is a product of the time it spent with its breeder, its genetic makeup and the guidance you have provided along the way.

If you are looking for a magic formula to picking the perfect pup you are going to be sadly disappointed. There is simply no such formula. People have been known to employ extensive selection processes that include so-called puppy temperament tests and field aptitude tests only to find out that what they selected just did not fit the bill in the long run. Others have been known to reach in and grab the first pup they see and have been highly successful in getting the perfect dog. Still, there are some general points to consider that might help your selection process.

Match your lifestyle to what you see in the pup. Are you sedentary and enjoy sitting in front of the fireplace with a good book on a cool autumn evening? Then you are best off picking the calm puppy that wants to curl up in your lap for a nice petting session while it chews on a bone. Do you enjoy a nice jog through the park rather than a leisurely walk around the block? Then the active pup is probably going to fit your situation better than any other. If you are some combination of these two, then go for the middle-of-the-road puppy.

People with children, especially small or active children, and first-time puppy buyers are best off picking the pup that tends to have a rather even (not too active or too laid-back) temperament. Likewise, the first-time puppy buyer and people with small or active children would do well to avoid any pup that seems to be demonstrating strong dominance tendencies while interacting with its littermates. It may go without saying, but the experienced dog owner who has been successful in owning and training other dogs can probably be successful and forge a good relationship with any of the personalities found in the puppies.

What happens if you contact a breeder and all that is left is one puppy? Do you take it or do you look elsewhere so that you or the breeder has a number of pups to choose from? The answer is, ask the breeder. Remember, you need to be able to trust the breeder you are working with. If the breeder is one that you trust, why would you not accept a pup from him just because it was the last one left in the litter? Most breeders do not want to have a puppy placement go bad. They want their pups to go to what is fondly referred to as a "forever home." A reputable breeder will not make a placement just to get the puppy out of the house and into someone else's hands, so you should be comfortable with accepting that last pup if it is offered to you.

Your puppy requires close supervision, as you never know what he's going to get into next.

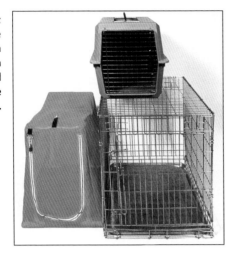

The three most common crate types: mesh on the left, wire on the right and fiberglass on the top.

When in doubt about which pup to pick, always rely on your breeder's insight and expertise. You will likely find that next to choosing a reputable breeder it was the best choice you could have made.

A COMMITTED NEW OWNER

By now you should understand what makes the AWS a most unique and special dog, one that may fit nicely into your family and lifestyle. If you have researched breeders, you should be able to recognize a knowledgeable and responsible AWS breeder who cares not only about his pups but also about what kind of owner you will be. If you have completed the final step in your new journey, you have found a litter, or possibly two, of quality AWS pups.

A visit with the puppies and their breeder should be an education in itself. Breed research, breeder selection and puppy visitation are very important aspects of finding the puppy of your dreams. Beyond that, these things also lay the foundation for a successful future with your pup. Puppy personalities within each litter vary, from the shy and easygoing puppy to the one who is dominant and assertive, with most pups falling somewhere in between. By spending time with the puppies you will be able to recognize certain behaviors and what these behaviors indicate about each pup's temperament. Which type of pup will complement your family dynamics is best determined by observing the puppies in action within their "pack." Your breeder's expertise and recommendations are also valuable. Although you may fall in love with a bold and brassy male, the breeder may suggest that another pup would be best for you. The breeder's experience in rearing AWS pups and matching their temperaments with appropriate humans offers the best assurance that your pup will meet your needs and expectations. The type of puppy that you select is just as important as your decision that the American Water Spaniel is the breed for you.

The decision to live with a AWS is a serious commitment and not one to be taken lightly. This puppy is a living sentient being that will be dependent on you for basic survival for his entire life. Beyond the basics of survival—food, water, shelter and protection—he needs much, much more. The new pup needs love, nurturing and a proper canine education to mold him into a responsible, well-behaved canine citizen. Your AWS's health and good manners will need consistent monitoring and regular "tune-ups," so your job as a responsible dog owner will be ongoing throughout every stage of his life. If you are not prepared to accept these responsibilities and commit to them for the next decade, likely longer, then you are not prepared to own a dog of any breed.

Although the responsibilities of owning a dog may at times tax your patience, the joy of living with your AWS far outweighs the workload, and a well-mannered adult dog is worth your time and effort. Before your very eyes, your new charge will grow up to be your most loyal friend, devoted to you unconditionally.

YOUR AWS SHOPPING LIST

Just as expectant parents prepare a nursery for their baby, so should you ready your home for the arrival of your AWS pup. If you have the necessary puppy supplies purchased and in place before he comes home, it will ease the puppy's transition from the warmth and familiarity of his mom and littermates to the brand-new environment of his new home and human family. You will be too busy to stock up and prepare your house after your pup comes home, that's for sure! Imagine how a pup must feel upon being transported to a strange new place. It's up to you to comfort him and to let your little pup know that he is going to be happy with you.

FOOD AND WATER BOWLS

Your puppy will need separate bowls for his food and water. Stainless steel pans are generally preferred over plastic bowls since they sterilize better and pups are less inclined to chew on the metal. Heavy-duty ceramic bowls are

Don't forget that the AWS is a hunting dog who specializes in birds. Owners who intend to work their dogs in the field introduce young puppies to game to give them the scent and sense of the hunt.

motels or at the vet's office; a training aid to help teach your puppy proper toileting habits; and a place of solitude when non-dog people happen to drop by and don't want a lively puppy—or even a well-behaved adult dog—saying hello or begging for attention.

Crates come in several types, although the wire crate and the fiberglass airline-type crate are the most popular. Both are safe and your puppy will adjust to either one, so the choice is up to you. The wire crates offer better visibility for the pup as well as better ventilation. Many of the wire crates easily collapse into suitcase-size carriers. The fiberglass crates, similar to those used by the airlines for animal transport, are sturdier and more den-like. However, the fiberglass crates do not collapse and are less ventilated than a wire crate, which can be problematic in hot weather. Some of the newer crates are made of heavy plastic mesh; they are very lightweight and fold up into slim-line suitcases. However, a mesh crate might not be suitable for a pup with manic chewing habits.

popular, but consider how often you will have to pick up those heavy bowls. Buy adult-sized pans, as your puppy will grow into them before you know it.

THE DOG CRATE

If you think that crates are tools of punishment and confinement for when a dog has misbehaved, think again. Most breeders and almost all trainers recommend a crate as the preferred house-training aid as well as for all-around puppy training and safety. Because dogs are natural den creatures that prefer cave-like environments, the benefits of crate use are many. The crate provides the puppy with his very own "safe house," a cozy place to sleep, take a break or seek comfort with a favorite toy; a travel aid to house your dog when on the road, at

Don't bother with a puppy-sized crate. Although your AWS will be a little fellow when you bring him home, he will grow up in the blink of an eye and your puppy crate will be useless. Purchase a crate that will accommodate an adult AWS. He will stand about 18 inches when full-grown, so a medium- to large-sized crate will fit him nicely.

BEDDING AND CRATE PADS

Your puppy will enjoy some type of soft bedding in his "room" (the crate), something he can snuggle into to feel cozy and secure. Old towels or blankets are good choices for a young pup, since he may (and probably will) have a toileting accident or two in the crate or decide to chew on the bedding material. Once he is fully trained and out of the early chewing stage, you can replace the puppy bedding with a permanent crate pad if you prefer. Crate pads and other dog beds run the gamut from inexpensive to high-end doggie-designer styles, but don't splurge on the good stuff until you are sure that your puppy is reliable and won't tear it up or make a mess on it.

PUPPY TOYS

Just as infants and older children require objects to stimulate their minds and bodies, puppies need toys to entertain their curious brains, wiggly paws and achy teeth. A fun array of safe doggie toys will

TOYS 'R SAFE

The vast array of tantalizing puppy toys is staggering. Stroll through any pet shop or pet-supply outlet and you will see that the choices can be overwhelming. However, not all dog toys are safe or sensible. Most very young puppies enjoy soft woolly toys that they can snuggle with and carry around. (You know they have outgrown them when they shred them up!) Avoid toys that have buttons, tabs or other enhancements that can be chewed off and swallowed. Soft toys that squeak are fun, but make sure your puppy does not disembowel the toy and remove (and swallow) the squeaker. Toys that rattle or make noise can excite a puppy, but they present the same danger as the squeaky kind and so require supervision. Hard rubber toys that bounce can also entertain a pup, but make sure that the toy is too big for your pup to swallow.

GOOD CHEWING

Chew toys run the gamut from rawhide chews to hard sterile bones and everything in between. Rawhides are all-time favorites, but they can cause choking when they become mushy from repeated chewing, causing them to break into small pieces that are easy to swallow. Rawhides are also highly indigestible, so many vets advise limiting rawhide treats. Hard sterile bones are great for plaque prevention as well as chewing satisfaction. Dispose of them when the ends become sharp or splintered.

help satisfy your puppy's chewing instincts and distract him from gnawing on the leg of your antique chair or your new leather sofa. Most puppy toys are cute and look as if they would be a lot of fun, but not all are necessarily safe or good for your puppy, so use caution when you go puppy-toy shopping.

Although American Water Spaniels are not known to be voracious chewers like many other dogs, they still love to chew, especially when bored or frustrated. The best "chewcifiers" are nylon and hard rubber bones, which are safe to gnaw on and come in sizes appropriate for all age groups and breeds. Be especially careful of natural bones, which can splinter or develop dangerous sharp edges; pups can easily swallow or choke on those bone splinters.

Veterinarians often tell of surgical nightmares involving bits of splintered bone, because in addition to the danger of choking, the sharp pieces can damage the intestinal tract.

Similarly, rawhide chews, while a favorite of most dogs and puppies, can be equally dangerous. Pieces of rawhide are easily swallowed after they get soft and gummy from chewing, and dogs have been known to choke on pieces of ingested rawhide. Rawhide chews should be offered only when you can supervise the puppy.

Soft woolly toys are special puppy favorites. They come in a wide variety of cute shapes and sizes; some look like little stuffed animals. Puppies love to shake them up and toss them about or simply carry them around. Be careful of fuzzy toys that have button eyes or noses that your pup could chew off and swallow, and make sure that he does not disembowel a squeaky toy to remove the squeaker! Braided rope toys are similar in that they are fun to chew and toss around, but they shred easily and the strings are easy to swallow. The strings are not digestible and, if the puppy doesn't pass them in his stool, he could end up at the vet's office. As with rawhides, your puppy should be closely monitored with rope toys.

If you believe that your pup has ingested one of these dangerous objects, check his stools for the next couple of days to see if he passes them when he defecates. At the same time, also watch for signs of intestinal distress. A call to your veterinarian might be in order to get his advice and be on the safe side.

An all-time favorite toy for puppies (young and old!) is the empty gallon milk jug. Hard plastic juice containers—46 ounces or more—are also excellent. Such containers make lots of noise when they are batted about, and puppies go crazy with delight as they play with them. However, they don't often last very long, so be sure to remove and replace them when they get chewed up on the ends.

A word of caution about homemade toys: be careful with your choices of non-traditional play objects. Never use old shoes or socks, since a puppy cannot distinguish between the old ones on which he's allowed to chew and the new ones in your closet that are strictly off limits. That principle applies to anything that resembles something that you don't want your puppy to chew.

COLLARS

A lightweight nylon collar is the best choice for a very young pup. Quick-click collars are easy to put on and remove, and they can be adjusted as the puppy grows. Introduce him to his collar as soon as he comes home to get him accustomed to wearing it. He'll get

KEEP OUT OF REACH

Most dogs don't browse around your medicine cabinet, but accidents do happen! The drug acetaminophen, the active ingredient in certain over-the-counter pain relievers, can be deadly to dogs and cats if ingested in large quantities. Acetaminophen toxicity, caused by the dog's swallowing 15 to 20 tablets, can be manifested in abdominal pains within a day or two of ingestion, as well as liver damage. If you suspect your dog has swiped a bottle of medication, get the dog to the vet immediately so that the vet can induce vomiting and cleanse the dog's stomach.

used to it quickly and won't mind a bit. Make sure that it is snug enough that it won't slip off yet loose enough to be comfortable for the pup. You should be able to slip two fingers between the collar and his neck. Check the collar often, as

A Dog-Safe Home

The dog-safety police are taking you and your new AWS puppy on a house tour. Let's go room by room and see how safe your own home is for your new pup. The following items are doggy dangers, so either they must be removed or the dog should be monitored or not allowed access to these areas.

Living Room

- house plants (some varieties are poisonous)
- fireplace or wood-burning stove
- paint on the walls (lead-based paint is toxic)
- lead drapery weights (toxic lead)
- lamps and electrical cords
- carpet cleaners or deodorizers

Outdoors

- swimming pool
- pesticides
- toxic plants
- lawn fertilizers

Bathroom

- blue water in the toilet bowl
- medicine cabinet (filled with potentially deadly bottles)
- soap bars, bleach, drain cleaners, etc.
- tampons

Kitchen

- household cleaners in the kitchen cabinets
- glass jars and canisters
- sharp objects (like kitchen knives, scissors and forks)
- garbage can (with remnants of good-smelling things like onions, potato skins, apple or pear cores, peach pits, coffee beans and other harmful tidbits)
- food left out on counters (some foods are toxic to dogs)

Garage

- antifreeze
- fertilizers (including rose foods)
- pesticides and rodenticides
- pool supplies (chlorine and other chemicals)
- oil and gasoline in containers
- sharp objects, electrical cords and power tools

puppies grow in spurts, and his collar can become too tight almost overnight. Choke collars are for training purposes only and should never be used on a puppy under four or five months old.

LEASHES

A 6-foot nylon lead is an excellent choice for a young puppy. It is lightweight and not as tempting to chew as a leather lead. You can switch to a 6-foot leather lead after your pup has grown and is used to walking politely on a lead. For initial puppy walks and house-training purposes, you should invest in a shorter lead so that you have more control over the puppy. At first, you don't want him wandering too far away from you, and when taking him out for toileting you will want to keep him in the specific area chosen for his potty spot.

Once the puppy is heel-trained with a traditional leash, you can consider purchasing a retractable lead. A retractable lead is excellent for walking adult dogs that are already leash-wise. This type of lead allows the dog to roam farther away from you and explore a wider area when out walking, and also retracts when you need to keep him close to you.

You can learn a lot about a puppy's future temperament by observing him at play with his littermates.

HOME SAFETY FOR YOUR PUPPY

The importance of puppy-proofing cannot be overstated. In addition to making your house comfortable for your AWS's arrival, you also must make sure that your house is safe for your puppy before you bring him home. There are countless hazards in the owner's personal living environment that a pup can sniff, chew, swallow or destroy. Many are obvious; others are not. Do a thorough advance house check to remove or rearrange those things

An orally-fixated AWS puppy finds just about anything chew-worthy. Keep an eye on what your dog puts into his mouth.

that could hurt your puppy, keeping any potentially dangerous items out of areas to which he will have access.

Electrical cords are especially dangerous, since puppies view them as irresistible chew toys. Unplug and remove all exposed cords or fasten them beneath baseboards where the puppy cannot reach them. Veterinarians and firefighters can tell you horror stories about electrical burns and house fires that resulted from puppy-chewed electrical cords. Consider this a most serious precaution for your puppy and the rest of your family.

Scout your home for tiny objects that might be seen at a pup's eye level. Keep medication bottles and cleaning supplies well out of reach, and do the same with waste baskets and other trash containers. It goes without saying that you should not use rodent poison or other toxic chemicals in any puppy area and that you must keep such containers safely locked up. You will be amazed at how many places a curious puppy can discover!

Once your house has cleared inspection, check your yard. A sturdy fence, well embedded into the ground, will give your dog a safe place to play and potty. Although American Water Spaniels are not known to be climbers or fence jumpers, they are still athletic dogs, so a 5- to 6-foot-high fence should be adequate to contain an agile youngster or adult. Check the fence periodically for necessary repairs. If there is a weak link or space to squeeze through, you can be sure a determined AWS will discover it.

The garage and shed can be hazardous places for a pup, as things like fertilizers, chemicals and tools are usually kept there. It's best to keep these areas off limits to the pup. Antifreeze is especially dangerous to dogs, as they find the taste appealing and it takes only a few licks from the driveway to kill a dog, puppy or adult, small breed or large.

ASK THE VET

Help your vet help you to become a well-informed dog owner. Don't be shy about becoming involved in your puppy's veterinary care by asking questions and gaining as much knowledge as you can. For starters, ask what shots your puppy is getting and what diseases they prevent, and discuss with your vet the safest way to vaccinate. Find out what is involved in your dog's annual wellness visits. If you plan to spay or neuter, discuss the best age at which to have this done. Start out on the right "paw" with your puppy's vet and develop good communication with him, as he will care for your dog's health throughout the dog's entire life.

VISITING THE VETERINARIAN

A good veterinarian is your AWS puppy's best health-insurance policy. If you do not already have a vet, ask friends and experienced dog people in your area for recommendations so that you can select a vet before you bring your AWS puppy home. Also arrange for your puppy's first veterinary examination beforehand, since many vets do not have appointments available immediately and your puppy should visit the vet within a day or so of coming home.

It's important to make sure your puppy's first visit to the vet is a pleasant and positive one. The vet should take great care to befriend the pup and handle him gently to make their first meeting a positive experience. The vet will give the pup a thorough physical examination and set up a schedule for vaccinations and other necessary wellness visits. Be sure to show your vet any health and inoculation records, which you should have received from your breeder. Your vet is a great source of canine health information, so be sure to ask questions and take notes. Creating a health journal for your puppy will make a handy reference for his wellness and any future health problems that may arise.

MEETING THE FAMILY

Your AWS's homecoming is an exciting time for all members of the family, and it's only natural that

Your pup may feel like a stranger in a strange land upon arrival at his new home. Don't worry; allow him to adapt at his own pace and he quickly will become one of the family.

everyone will be eager to meet him, pet him and play with him. However, for the puppy's sake, it's best to make these initial family meetings as uneventful as possible so that the pup is not overwhelmed with too much too soon. Remember, he has just left his dam and his littermates and is away from the breeder's home for the first time. Despite his fuzzy wagging tail, he is still apprehensive and wondering where he is and who all these strange humans are. It's best to let him explore on his own and meet the family members as he feels comfortable. Let him investigate all the new smells, sights and sounds at his own pace. Children should be especially careful to not get overly excited, use loud voices or hug the pup too tightly. Be calm, gentle and affectionate, and be ready to comfort him if he appears frightened or uneasy.

Be sure to show your puppy his new crate during this first day home. Toss a treat or two inside the crate; if he associates the crate with food, he will associate the crate with good things. If he is comfortable with the crate, you can offer him his first meal inside it. Leave the door ajar so he can wander in and out as he chooses.

FIRST NIGHT IN HIS NEW HOME
So much has happened in your AWS puppy's first day away from the breeder. He's likely had his first car ride to his new home. He's met his new human family and perhaps the other family pets. He has explored his new house and yard, at least those places where he is to be allowed during his first weeks at

> ## SOCIALIZATION PERIOD
> Canine research has shown that a puppy's 8th through 20th week is the most critical learning period of his life. This is when the puppy "learns to learn," a time when he needs positive experiences to build confidence and stability. Puppies who are not exposed to different people and situations outside the home during this period can grow up to be fearful and sometimes aggressive. This is also the best time for puppy lessons, since he has not yet acquired any bad habits that could undermine his ability to learn.

home. He may have visited his new veterinarian. He has eaten his first meal or two away from his dam and littermates. Surely that's enough to tire out an eight-week-old AWS pup—or so you hope!

It's bedtime. During the day, the pup investigated his crate, which is his new den and sleeping space, so it is not entirely strange to him. Line the crate with a soft towel or blanket that he can snuggle into and gently place him into the crate for the night. Some breeders send home a piece of bedding from where the pup slept with his littermates, and those familiar scents are a great comfort for the puppy on his first night without his siblings.

He will probably whine or cry. The puppy is objecting to the confinement and the fact that he is alone for the first time. This can be

When you bring your AWS puppy home, everything will be new to him. Give him time to explore and get used to all of the sights, scents and sounds.

Crate and barrel! A gorgeous litter of American Water Spaniels puppies poses for a family portrait.

a stressful time for you as well as for the pup. It's important that you remain strong and don't let the puppy out of his crate to comfort him. He will fall asleep eventually. If you release him, the puppy will learn that crying means "out" and will continue that habit. You are laying the groundwork for future habits. Some breeders find that soft music can soothe a crying pup and help him get to sleep.

SOCIALIZING YOUR PUPPY

The first 20 weeks of your AWS puppy's life are the most important of his entire lifetime. A properly socialized puppy will grow up to be a confident and stable adult who will be a pleasure to live with and a welcome addition to the neighborhood.

The importance of socialization cannot be overemphasized. Research on canine behavior has proven that puppies who are not exposed to new sights, sounds, people and animals during their first 20 weeks of life will grow up to be timid and fearful, even aggressive, and unable to flourish outside of their home environment.

Socializing your puppy is not difficult and, in fact, will be a fun time for you both. Lead training goes hand in hand with socialization, so your puppy will be learning how to walk on a lead at the same time that he's meeting the neighborhood. Because the AWS is such a wonderful breed, everyone will enjoy meeting "the new kid on the block." Take him for short walks to the park and to other dog-friendly places where he will encounter new people, especially children. Puppies automatically recognize children as "little people" and are drawn to play with them. Just make sure that you supervise these meetings and that the children do not get too rough or encourage him to play too hard. An overzealous pup can often nip too hard, frightening the child and in turn making the puppy overly excited. A bad experience in puppyhood can impact a dog for life, so a pup that has a negative experience with a

child may grow up to be shy or even aggressive around children.

Take your puppy along on your daily errands. Puppies are natural "people magnets," and most people who see your pup will want to pet him. All of these encounters will help to mold him into a confident adult dog. Likewise, you will soon feel like a confident, responsible dog owner, rightly proud of your handsome AWS.

Be especially careful of your puppy's encounters and experiences during the eight-to-ten-week-old period, which is also called the "fear period." This is a serious imprinting period, and all contact during this time should be gentle and positive. A frightening or negative event could leave a permanent impression that could affect his future behavior if a similar situation arises.

Also make sure that your puppy has received his first and second rounds of vaccinations before you expose him to other dogs or bring him to places that other dogs may frequent. Avoid dog parks and other strange-dog areas until your vet assures you that your puppy is fully immunized and resistant to the diseases that can be passed between canines. Discuss socialization with your breeder, as some breeders recommend socializing the puppy even before he has received all of his inoculations, depending on how outgoing the individul puppy may be.

Your AWS puppy will look to you to provide him with the care and love that he requires and deserves.

LEADER OF THE PUPPY'S PACK
Like other canines, your puppy needs an authority figure, someone he can look up to and regard as the leader of his "pack." His first pack leader was his dam, who taught him to be polite and not chew too hard on her ears or nip at her muzzle. He learned those same lessons from his litter-mates. If he played too rough, they cried in pain and stopped the game, which sent an important message to the rowdy puppy.

As puppies play together, they are also struggling to determine who will be the boss. Being pack animals, dogs need someone to be in charge. If a litter of puppies remained together beyond puppyhood, one of the pups would emerge as the strongest one, the one who calls the shots.

Once your puppy leaves the pack, he will look intuitively for a new leader. If he does not recognize you as that leader, he will try to assume that position for himself. Of course, it is hard to imagine your adorable AWS puppy trying to be in charge when he is so small and seemingly helpless. You must remember that these are natural canine instincts. Do not cave in and allow your pup to get the upper "paw"!

Just as socialization is so important during these first 20 weeks, so too is your puppy's early education. He was born without any bad habits. He does not know what is good or bad behavior. If he does things like nipping and digging, it's because he is having

fun and doesn't know that humans consider these things as "bad." It's your job to teach him proper puppy manners, and this is the best time to accomplish that—before he has developed bad habits, since it is much more difficult to "unlearn" or correct unacceptable learned

Your puppy will also look to you, as the pack leader, to set the rules and boundaries. If you don't, he will make his own rules.

Through play, littermates determine their place in the pack—with you always on top.

behavior than to teach good behavior from the start.

Make sure that all members of the family understand the importance of being consistent when training their new puppy. If you tell the puppy to stay off the sofa and your daughter allows him to cuddle on the couch to watch her favorite television show, your pup will be confused about what he is and is not allowed to do. Have a family conference before your pup comes home so that everyone understands the basic principles of puppy training and the rules you have set forth for the pup and agrees to follow them.

The old saying that "an ounce of prevention is worth a pound of cure" is especially true when it comes to puppies. It is much easier to prevent inappropriate behavior than it is to change it. It's also easier and less stressful for the pup, since it will keep discipline to a minimum and create a more positive learning environment for him. That, in turn, will also be easier on you!

Here are a few commonsense tips to keep your belongings safe and your puppy out of trouble:

- Keep your closet doors closed and your shoes, socks and other apparel off the floor so your puppy can't get at them.
- Keep a secure lid on the trash container or put the trash where your puppy can't dig into it. He can't damage what he can't reach!
- Supervise your puppy at all times to make sure he is not getting into mischief. If he starts to chew the corner of the rug, you can distract him instantly by tossing a toy for him to fetch. You also will be able to whisk him outside when you notice that he is about to piddle on the carpet. If you can't see your puppy, you can't teach him or correct his behavior.

SOLVING PUPPY PROBLEMS

CHEWING AND NIPPING
Nipping at fingers and toes is normal puppy behavior. Chewing is also the way that puppies investigate their surroundings. However, you will have to teach your puppy that chewing anything other than

Familiarizing your AWS with game at a young age will be a good start to field training.

his toys is not acceptable. That won't happen overnight and at times puppy teeth will test your patience. However, if you allow nipping and chewing to continue, just think about the damage that a mature AWS can do with a full set of adult teeth.

Whenever your puppy nips your hand or fingers, cry out "Ouch!" in a loud voice, which should startle your puppy and stop him from nipping, even if only for a moment. Immediately distract him by offering a small treat or an appropriate toy for him to chew instead (which means having chew toys and puppy treats handy or in your pockets at all times). Praise him when he takes the toy, and tell him what a good fellow he is. Praise is just as or even more important in puppy training as discipline and correction.

Puppies also tend to nip at children more often than adults, since they perceive little ones to be more vulnerable and more similar to their littermates. Teach your children appropriate responses to nipping behavior. If they are unable to handle it themselves, you may

"Why doesn't this duck fly away from us?"

have to intervene. Puppy nips can be quite painful and a child's frightened reaction will only encourage a puppy to nip harder, which is a natural canine response. As with all other puppy situations, interaction between your AWS puppy and children should be supervised.

Chewing on objects, not just family members' fingers and ankles, is also normal canine behavior that can be especially tedious (for the owner, not the pup) during the teething period when the puppy's adult teeth are coming in. At this stage, chewing just plain feels good. Furniture legs and cabinet corners are common puppy favorites. Shoes

BE CONSISTENT

Consistency is a key element, in fact is absolutely necessary, to a puppy's learning environment. A behavior (such as chewing, jumping up or climbing onto the furniture) cannot be forbidden one day and then allowed the next. That will only confuse the pup, and he will not understand what he is supposed to do. Just one or two episodes of allowing an undesirable behavior to "slide" will imprint that behavior on a puppy's brain and make that behavior more difficult to erase or change.

"Did I do something wrong?" Your AWS puppy will test you with his behavior. Be sure to let him know what is and is not allowed.

and other personal items also taste pretty good to a pup.

The best solution is, once again, prevention. If you value something, keep it tucked away and out of reach. You can't hide your dining-room table in a closet, but you can try to deflect the chewing by applying a bitter product made just to deter dogs from chewing. Available in a spray or cream, this substance is vile-tasting, although safe for dogs, and most puppies will avoid the forbidden object after one tiny taste. You also can apply the product to your leather leash if the puppy tries to chew on his lead during leash-training sessions.

Keep a ready supply of safe chews handy to offer your AWS as a distraction when he starts to chew on something that's a "no-no."

Remember, at this tender age he does not yet know what is permitted or forbidden, so you have to be "on call" every minute he's awake and on the prowl.

You may lose a treasure or two during your puppy's growing-up period, and the furniture could sustain a nasty nick or two. These can be trying times, so be prepared for those inevitable accidents and comfort yourself in knowing that this too shall pass.

PUPPY WHINING

Puppies often cry and whine, just as infants and little children do. It's their way of telling us that they are lonely or in need of attention. Your puppy will miss his littermates and will feel insecure when he is left alone.

You may be out of the house or just in another room, but he will still feel alone. During these times, the puppy's crate should be his personal comfort station, a place all his own where he can feel safe and secure. Once he learns that being alone is okay and not something to be feared, he will settle down without crying or objecting. You might want to leave a radio on while he is crated, as the sound of human voices can be soothing and will give the impression that people are around.

Give your American Water Spaniel puppy a favorite cuddly toy or chew toy to entertain him whenever he is crated. You will both be happier: the puppy because he is safe in his den and you because he is quiet, safe and not getting into puppy escapades

that can wreak havoc in your house or cause him danger.

To make sure that your puppy will always view his crate as a safe and cozy place, never, *ever* use the crate as punishment. That's the best way to turn the crate into a negative place that the pup will want to avoid. Sure, you can use the crate for your own peace of mind if your puppy is getting into trouble and needs some "time out." Just don't let him know that. Never scold the pup and immediately place him into the crate. Count to ten, give him a couple of hugs and maybe a treat, then scoot him into his crate.

It's also important not to make a big fuss when he is released from the crate. That will make getting out of the crate more appealing than being in the crate, which is just the opposite of what you are trying to achieve.

Puppies are normally go, go, go but when it's time for a nap, their world comes to a grinding halt.

AMERICAN WATER SPANIEL

Adding an AWS to your household means adding a new family member who will need your care each and every day. When your AWS pup first comes home, you will start a routine with him so that, as he grows up, your dog will have a daily schedule just as you do. The aspects of your dog's daily care will likewise become regular parts of your day, so you'll both have a new schedule. Dogs learn by consistency and thrive on routine: regular times for meals, exercise, grooming and potty trips are just as important for your dog as they are for you. Your dog's schedule will depend much on your family's daily routine, but remember that

Pups get the best start in life from nursing from their mother. It's hard work being mom to a hungry litter.

HOLD THE ONIONS & MORE

Sliced, chopped, grated; dehydrated, boiled, fried or raw; pearl, Spanish, white or red: onions can be deadly to your dog. The toxic effects of onions in dogs are cumulative for up to 30 days. A serious form of anemia, called Heinz body anemia, affects the red blood cells of dogs that have eaten onions. For safety (and better breath), dogs should avoid chives and scallions as well.

Small amounts of fresh grapes and raisins can cause vomiting and diarrhea in dogs, possibly even kidney failure in the worst cases. Nuts, in general, are not recommended for dogs. Macadamia nuts, for example, can cause vomiting, diarrhea, fatigue and temporary paralysis of rear legs. Dogs usually recover from these symptoms in a few days. Almonds are also especially problematic for dogs.

you now have a new member of the family who is part of your day every day!

FEEDING
Before you bring your puppy home from the breeder, check to find out what type of food the breeder has

been feeding. Also ask about how much food the puppy should be fed each day or at each feeding to ease the transition into the new home. If you are going to switch the puppy to a different food once you have gotten it home, you should do so gradually. Pick up a small package of the food that the breeder is feeding and slowly mix the two foods together. Begin the change to the new food gradually, beginning with a higher percentage of the breeder's recommendation and gradually changing to a higher percentage of the new product. After about two weeks the pup should be completely switched over to the new food with no problem.

There is a large debate about whether a puppy should be on a puppy food until it is a year old, six months old or even whether it should have puppy food at all. It is probably best to consult both your breeder and your veterinarian about what is best, but ultimately you will have to make the decision yourself. If you do decide to feed puppy food, once the time comes to change to an adult product you will normally not have to follow the procedure of gradually mixing the two, especially if you stay with the same product manufacturer.

Most breeders and veterinarians recommend that you feed a premium food product rather than a "grocery-store" brand. There are many premium products on the

Dinnertime! This litter shares a "family-style" meal as they begin to eat solid food.

market that offer a full line of life-stage foods beginning with puppy food and going through to senior diets. Finding where to get such foods is normally no more difficult than locating your nearest specialty pet store or consulting your veterinarian. Premium foods are, pound for pound, higher in nutritional value and have less fillers than non-premium types. These foods are normally formulated to maintain a quality coat and reduce tartar build-up on the teeth. The quality nutrition and reduced filler will work together to reduce the quantity of stool produced by the dog and will make clean up much easier, while maintaining a healthy dog.

The American Water Spaniel is a breed that likes to eat, so be conservative in the quantity of food you provide. Be certain to fulfill your dog's requirements, but if you notice the dog is putting on a few

Though your AWS will always prefer his food, water must be available to wash it all down.

A sporting breed like the AWS will need water after time spent working in the field.

extra pounds, reduce the amount fed and increase its exercise a bit. A fat dog is not a healthy dog, and studies have shown that your dog will live longer if it is a little underweight rather than a little overweight.

DON'T FORGET THE WATER!
For a dog, it's always time for a drink! Regardless of what type of food he eats, there's no doubt that he needs plenty of water. Fresh cold water, in a clean bowl, should be freely available to your dog at all times. There are special circumstances, such as during puppy housebreaking, when you will want to monitor your pup's water intake so that you will be able to predict when he will need to relieve himself, but water must be available to him nonetheless. Water is essential for hydration and proper body function just as it is in humans.

You will get to know how much your dog typically drinks in a day. Of course, in the heat, in the field or if exercising vigorously, he will be more thirsty and will drink more. However, if he begins to drink noticeably more water for no apparent reason, this could signal any of various problems, and you are advised to consult your vet.

Water is the best drink for dogs. Some owners are tempted to give milk from time to time or to moisten dry food with milk, but dogs do not have the enzymes necessary to digest the lactose in milk, which is much different from the milk that nursing puppies receive. Therefore stick with clean fresh water to quench your dog's thirst, and always have it readily available to him.

QUENCHING HIS THIRST

Is your dog drinking more than normal and trying to lap up everything in sight? Excessive drinking has many different causes. Obvious causes for a dog's being thirstier than usual are hot weather and vigorous exercise. However, if your dog is drinking more for no apparent reason, you could have cause for concern. Serious conditions like kidney or liver disease, diabetes and various types of hormonal problems can all be indicated by excessive drinking. If you notice your dog's being excessively thirsty, contact your vet at once. Hopefully there will be a simpler explanation, but the earlier a serious problem is detected, the sooner it can be treated, with a better rate of cure.

EXERCISE

Like most sporting or hunting dogs, the American Water Spaniel is an active breed with an insatiable appetite for work. A good exercise program is essential to maintaining a physically fit and rather calm AWS. Jogging, walking, hiking and swimming are some of the more common exercise programs used to keep the AWS in top physical condition. As a medium-sized breed the AWS will do fine with a varied but consistent level of activity that provides approximately 20 to 30 minutes of exercise once or twice a day. Working a training program into the time set aside for exercise will allow the owner to exercise the dog's mind and body in a way that will not impinge too much on an owner's busy lifestyle.

For the young puppy a prolonged exercise period is less desirable due to the possible stress it can place on the dog's growing body. In the beginning a pup will do fine with short periods of exercise that are gradually lengthened as the pup matures. Taking a young pup for a leisurely walk through the field or letting it explore along the water's edge is a good way of helping it to both exercise and become comfortable with new environments.

GROOMING

The American Water Spaniel is considered by most to be a breed that requires just a moderate amount of grooming. Daily brushing will certainly help to reduce shedding and keep a healthy coat, but in most cases it is not necessary. However, weekly brushing should occur along with

Daily exercise is an absolute must for this sporting breed, and he will thank you with a smile for allowing him the time to work off that energy.

PUPPY STEPS

Puppies are brimming with activity and enthusiasm. It seems that they can play all day and night without tiring, but don't overdo your puppy's exercise regimen. Easy does it for the puppy's first six to nine months. Keep walks brief and don't let the puppy engage in stressful jumping games. The puppy frame is delicate, and too much exercise during those critical growing months can cause injury to his bone structure, ligaments and musculature. Save his first jog for his first birthday!

a good "going over" to remove burs and other debris gathered during a romp in the field.

When it comes to the type of equipment to have available, it is suggested that you start with a combination of a pin brush, a slicker brush and a strong comb. A good pair of shears is needed and, unless you are experienced with dog shears and trimming dogs, you should start with a pair of blunt-nose shears to avoid accidentally poking your dog as you groom him. While not absolutely necessary, it can also be helpful to keep a pair of thinning shears on hand. These will help to remove any mats that may form in the dog's coat between brushings. A pair of nail clippers will be needed to keep the nails neatly trimmed. There are two common types of nail clippers: the guillotine and the heavy-duty trimmer. The author prefers the trimmer, but the inexperienced owner is probably better off with the guillotine clipper, which has a design that helps to hold the nail in place as you clip it. It is always good to keep a bottle of styptic powder on hand just in case you clip a nail a little too short and cut the quick (more about this later).

If you are going to groom your dog, you should find a raised surface like a table or countertop on which to work. You can actually buy grooming tables designed just for this purpose, but for the average owner it is probably not necessary. Any raised surface that provides secure footing for your dog and allows you to move freely around the dog will work fine.

Grooming should begin with a thorough brushing of the coat to remove debris and mats. Brush out the body area first and then proceed to the backs of the legs, the tail and finally the ears. Following this order will help to avoid starting out with brushing what can be a more stressful area, like the ears, first and will ease the dog into the process. In general you will use the pin brush for the more sparsely coated dogs and the slicker brush for dogs that are heavier coated. Also use the pin brush for removing dead under-coat, mats and burs. The ears tend to be the area that collects the most debris. For this reason you should first comb through them, locating problem areas and removing any unwanted tangles. Then brush through using either the slicker or pin brush.

Once brushed the dog should be thoroughly bathed with a quality doggie shampoo. This will remove the dirt and excess oil from the coat and therefore help to keep your shears sharp. Many AWS owners use a bronzing shampoo with natural hennas to bring out the lustrous beauty of the brown coat.

Once he is bathed and dried off, brush the dog again just as was described earlier. Again, it is suggested that you begin with the body of the dog rather than the more stressful head area. The body coat will often grow somewhat unevenly, so even it up to a more uniform length. The feathering on the legs can be evened to a more equal length along the entire leg. Holding the tail outward, observe its general appearance. If it is feathered consider shaping the feathers into a rocker shape as is

Be sure the grooming tools you use are sturdy and afford a comfortable grip.

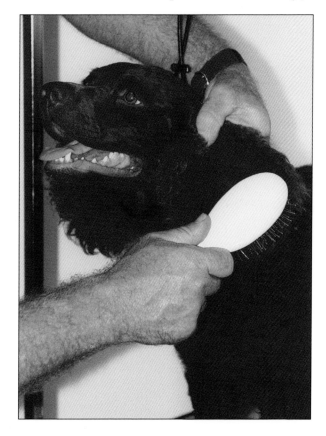

Selecting the Right Brushes and Combs

Will a rubber curry make my dog look slicker? Is a rake smaller than a pin brush? Do I choose nylon or natural bristles? Buying a dog brush can make the hairs on your head stand on end! Here's a quick once-over to educate you on the different types of brushes.

Slicker Brush: Fine metal prongs closely set on a curved base. Used to remove dead coat from the undercoat of medium- to long-coated breeds.

Pin Brush: Metal pins, often covered with rubber tips, set on an oval base. Used to remove shedding hair and is gentler than a slicker brush.

Metal Comb: Steel teeth attached to a steel handle; the closeness and size of the teeth vary greatly. A "flea comb" has tiny teeth set very closely together and is used to find fleas in a dog's coat. Combs with wider teeth are used for detangling longer coats.

Rake: Long-toothed comb with a short handle. Used to remove undercoat from heavily coated breeds with dense undercoats.

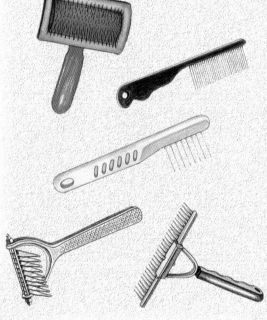

Soft-bristle Brush: Nylon or natural bristles set in a plastic or wood base. Used on short coats or long coats (without undercoats).

Rubber Curry: Rubber prongs, with or without a handle. Used for short-coated dogs. Good for use during shampooing.

Combination Brushes: Two-sided brush with a different type of bristle on each side; for example, pin brush on one side and slicker on the other, or bristle brush on one side and pin brush on the other. An economical choice if you need two kinds of brushes.

Grooming Glove: Sometimes called a hound glove; used to give sleek-coated dogs a once-over.

called for in the breed standard. If the tail is covered in curls, you will probably only have to even the curls up much like you did with the body. In an effort to prevent a build-up of debris, many groomers will trim the hair on the tail a little shorter at its base.

Moving to the feet, brush backward from the nails toward the leg and draw the hair between the toes upward; you can also use your fingers to pull this hair up if the brush is not adequate. Now take your shears and trim the hair down to a level that is even with the top of the toes. This will give a neat appearance to the foot and reduce the amount of mud and debris the dog will pick up on its daily romps. American Water Spaniels have very hairy feet, so trim around the outer edges of the foot as well so that the hair is short to the sides of the pads. Turn the foot over and trim the hair from the bottom of the foot.

Brush the hair on the back of the pasterns and hocks outward, and then trim either close to the body or even with the rest of the feathering on the legs. If you trim close to the body, you will reduce the amount of debris brought into the house. Trimming the hair even with the rest of the feathering on the leg will make for a neat appearance and make the leg look fuller, having more substance.

Brush the ears thoroughly and then begin by removing excess hair from under the ear flap and around the ear canal. Keeping this area free of excess hair will allow for greater air flow and help the ear canal dry out after a swim. Right below the ear canal and against the head is an area of hair referred to as the "sideburns." This is a thick growth of hair that forms and should be clipped short to prevent matting and other problems from forming around the ear.

Before trimming the top of the ear, brush the top of the head and remove any topknot or excessive curls from the top of the skull or forehead. If you wish to leave these because you find them attractive then do so, but most people like to trim the top of the head and skull so that it has a smoother appearance. Some groomers will trim the hair on the ear short from the base of the ear to about a quarter

The crisp, curly coat of the AWS is a defining feature of this field dog.

to one-third of the way down the ear. Others will simply let it stay long, trimming away only the unruly strands that appear. It is really a matter of personal choice, so you may wish to experiment once or twice to see which you prefer. Shape the ear into a pendulum shape and even the length of the two ears up so that they are equal.

Some owners choose to take a simpler approach to grooming. Once or twice a year they will send the dog to the groomer and have a full-body cut done on the dog. Usually the groomer will use a #4 or #5 blade on an electric clipper and trim the dog all over to one uniform length. The ears and the feet will still have to be done as described earlier, but this is a good cut for a dog that is not going into the show ring, being used for cold-water retrieving any time soon or is suffering from the heat of summer. It does not take long for the coat to grow out again, so a dog trimmed like this in July will be sufficiently coated by the time cold weather sets in around late October or early November.

BATHING

In general, dogs need to be bathed only a few times a year, possibly more often if your dog gets into something messy or if he starts to smell like a dog. Show dogs are usually bathed before every show, which could be as frequent as weekly, although this depends on the owner. Bathing too frequently can have negative effects on the skin and coat, removing natural oils and causing dryness.

If you give your dog his first bath when he is young, he will become accustomed to the process. Wrestling a dog into the tub or chasing a freshly shampooed dog who has escaped from the bath will be no fun! Most dogs don't naturally enjoy their baths, but you at least want yours to cooperate with you.

Before bathing the dog, have the items you'll need close at hand. First, decide where you will bathe the dog. You should have a tub or basin with a non-slip surface. Puppies can even be bathed in a sink. In warm weather, some like to use a portable pool in the yard, although you'll want to make sure your dog doesn't head for the nearest dirt pile following his bath. You will also need a hose or shower spray to wet the coat thoroughly, a shampoo formulated for dogs, absorbent towels and perhaps a blow dryer. Human shampoos are too harsh for dogs' coats and will dry them out.

Before wetting the dog, give him a brush-through to remove any dead hair, dirt and mats.

Make sure he is at ease in the tub and have the water at a comfortable temperature. Begin bathing by wetting the coat all the way down to the skin. Massage in the shampoo, keeping it away from his face and eyes. Rinse him thoroughly, again avoiding the eyes and ears, as you don't want to get water into the ear canals. A thorough rinsing is important, as shampoo residue is drying and itchy to the dog. After rinsing, wrap him in a towel to absorb the initial moisture. You can finish drying with either a towel or a blow dryer on low heat, held at a safe distance from the dog. You should keep the dog indoors and away from drafts until he is completely dry.

NAIL CLIPPING

Nail clipping can often be a challenge with an AWS, so patience and frequency help a lot. Begin trimming your dog's nails at an early age and start by just doing one or two nails a day followed by a treat for good behavior. Gradually, over time, you just may get your dog to enjoy having his nails done. Take just enough of the nail off to keep the nail from contacting the surface while the dog is standing. If your dog's nails are very long to begin with you may need to take a little bit of the nail off over several sessions

WATER SHORTAGE
No matter how well behaved your dog is, bathing is always a project! Nothing can substitute for a good warm bath, but owners do have the option of giving their dogs "dry" baths. Pet shops sell excellent products, in both powder and spray forms, designed for spot-cleaning your dog. These dry shampoos are convenient for touch-up jobs when you don't have the time to bathe your dog in the traditional way.

Muddy feet, messy behinds and smelly coats can be spot-cleaned and deodorized with a "wet-nap"-style cleaner. On those days when your dog insists on rolling in fresh goose droppings and there's no time for a bath, a spot bath can save the day. These pre-moistened wipes are also handy for other grooming needs like wiping faces, ears and eyes and freshening tails and behinds.

before you have gotten it to the proper length. Long nails can cause the dog's feet to spread, which is not good for him; likewise, long nails can hurt if they unintentionally scratch, not good for you!

Some dogs' nails are worn down naturally by regular walking on hard surfaces, so the frequency with which you clip depends on your individual dog. Look at his nails from time to time and clip as needed; a good way to know when it's time for a trim is if you hear your dog

Special nail clippers designed for use on dogs are available at pet-supply stores.

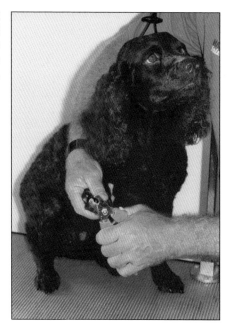

opening, and blades on the top and bottom snip it off in one clip.

Start by grasping the pup's paw; a little pressure on the foot pad causes the nail to extend, making it easier to clip. Clip off a little at a time. If you can see the "quick," which is a blood

clicking as he walks across the floor.

There are several types of nail clippers and even electric nail-grinding tools made for dogs; first we'll discuss using the clipper. To start, have your clipper ready and some doggie treats on hand. You want your pup to view his nail-clipping sessions in a positive light, and what better way to convince him than with food? You may want to enlist the help of an assistant to comfort the pup and offer treats as you concentrate on the clipping itself. The guillotine-type clipper is thought of by many as the easiest type to use; the nail tip is inserted into the

THE MONTHLY GRIND

If your dog doesn't like the feeling of nail clippers or if you're not comfortable using them, you may wish to try an electric nail grinder. This tool has a small sandpaper disc on the end that rotates to grind the nails down. Some feel that using a grinder reduces the risk of cutting into the quick; this can be true if the tool is used properly. Usually you will be able to tell where the quick is before you get to it. A benefit of the grinder is that it creates a smooth finish on the nails so that there are no ragged edges.

Because the tool makes noise, your dog should be introduced to it before the actual grinding takes place. Turn it on and let your dog hear the noise; turn it off and let him inspect it with you holding it. Use the grinder gently, holding it firmly and progressing a little at a time until you reach the proper length. Look at the nail as you grind so that you do not go too short. Stop at any indication that you are nearing the quick. It will take a few sessions for both you and the puppy to get used to the grinder. Make sure that you don't let his hair get tangled in the grinder!

vessel that runs through each nail, you will know how much to trim, as you do not want to cut into the quick. On that note, if you do cut the quick, which will cause bleeding, you can stem the flow of blood with a styptic pencil or other clotting agent. If you mistakenly nip the quick, do not panic or fuss, as this will cause the pup to be afraid. Simply reassure the pup, stop the bleeding and move on to the next nail. Don't be discouraged; you will become a professional canine pedicurist with practice.

You may or may not be able to see the quick, so it's best to just clip off a small bit at a time. If you see a dark dot in the center of the nail, this is the quick and your cue to stop clipping. Tell the puppy he's a "good boy" and offer a piece of treat with each nail. You can also use nail-clipping time to examine the footpads, making sure that they are not dry and cracked and that nothing has become embedded in them.

The nail grinder, the other choice, is many owners' first choice. Accustoming the puppy to the sound of the grinder and sensation of the buzz presents fewer challenges than the clipper, and there's no chance of cutting through the quick. Use the grinder on a low setting and always talk soothingly to your

dog. He won't mind his salon visit, and he'll have nicely polished nails as well.

If you are in doubt about what to do, ask your veterinarian or a local groomer to show you exactly how it is properly done.

EAR CLEANING

While keeping your dog's ears clean unfortunately will not cause him to "hear" your commands any better, it will protect him from ear infection

TOP: The ears should be cleaned with a soft cotton ball or wipe, but never probe into your dog's ear. BOTTOM: An ear-cleaning solution can be used to assist in the cleaning process, keeping the ears free of dirt and waxy build-up.

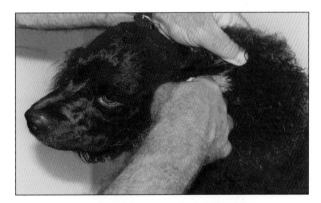

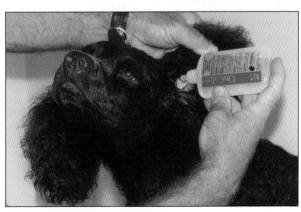

For a field dog, it is essential to make sure that the eyes are clear of debris and healthy looking.

solutions with ingredients like one part white vinegar and one part hydrogen peroxide. Ask your vet about home remedies before you attempt to concoct something on your own.

Keep your dog's ears free of excess hair by plucking it as needed. If done gently, this will be painless for the dog. Look for wax, brown droppings (a sign of ear mites), redness or any other abnormalities. At the first sign of a problem, contact your vet so that he can prescribe an appropriate medication.

and ear-mite infestation. In addition, a dog's ears are vulnerable to waxy build-up and to collecting foreign matter from the outdoors. Look in your dog's ears regularly to ensure that they look pink, clean and otherwise healthy. Even if they look fine, an odor in the ears signals a problem and means it's time to call the vet.

A dog's ears should be cleaned regularly; once a week is suggested, and you can do this along with your regular brushing. Using a cotton ball or pad, and never probing into the ear canal, wipe the ear gently. You can use an ear-cleansing liquid or powder available from your vet or pet-supply store; alternatively, you might prefer to use homemade

EYE CARE

During grooming sessions, pay extra attention to the condition of your dog's eyes. If the area around the eyes is soiled or if tear staining has occurred, there are various cleaning agents made especially for this purpose. Look at the dog's eyes to make sure no debris has entered; dogs with large eyes and those who spend time outdoors are especially prone to this.

The signs of an eye infection are obvious: mucus, redness,

puffiness, scabs or other signs of irritation. If your dog's eyes become infected, the vet will likely prescribe an antibiotic ointment for treatment. If you notice signs of more serious problems, such as opacities in the eye, which usually indicate cataracts, consult the vet at once. Taking time to pay attention to your dog's eyes will alert you in the early stages of any problem so that you can get your dog treatment as soon as possible. You could save your dog's sight.

A CLEAN SMILE

Another essential part of grooming is brushing your dog's teeth and checking his overall oral condition. Studies show that around 80% of dogs experience dental problems by 2 years of age, and the percentage is higher in older dogs. Therefore it is highly likely that your dog will have trouble with his teeth and gums unless you are proactive with home dental care.

The most common dental problem in dogs is plaque build-up. If not treated, this causes gum disease, infection and resultant tooth loss. Bacteria from these infections spread throughout the body, affecting the vital organs. Do you need much more convincing to start brushing your dog's teeth? If so, take a good whiff of your dog's breath and read on.

Fortunately, home dental care is rather easy and convenient for pet owners. Specially formulated canine toothpaste is easy to find. You should use one of these toothpastes, not a product for humans. Some doggie pastes are even available in flavors appealing to dogs. If your dog likes the flavor, he will tolerate the process better, making things

TOP: Examine your dog's teeth on a regular basis, at least weekly. BOTTOM: Scaling or scraping the dog's teeth removes tartar and plaque. Your veterinarian is best qualified to perform this task.

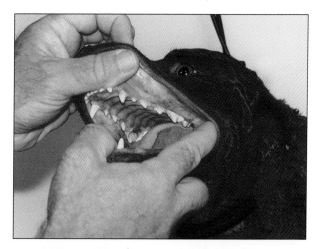

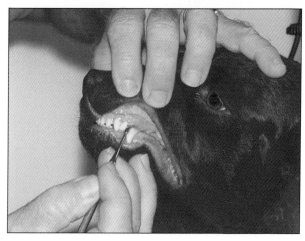

much easier for you. Doggie toothbrushes come in different sizes and are designed to fit the contour of a canine mouth. Rubber fingertip brushes fit right on one of your fingers and have rubber nodes to clean the teeth and massage the gums. This may be easier to handle, as it is akin to rubbing your dog's teeth with your finger.

As with other grooming tasks, accustom your AWS pup to his dental care early on. Start gently, for a few minutes at a time, so that he gets used to the feel of the brush and to your handling his mouth. Offer praise and petting so that he looks at tooth-care time as a time when he gets extra love and attention. The routine should

SCOOTING HIS BOTTOM

Here's a doggy problem that many owners tend to neglect. If your dog is scooting his rear end around the carpet, he probably is experiencing anal-sac impaction or blockage. The anal sacs are the two grape-sized glands on either side of the dog's vent. The dog cannot empty these glands, which become filled with a foul-smelling material. The dog may attempt to lick the area to relieve the pressure. He may also rub his anus on your walls, furniture or floors.

Don't neglect your dog's rear end during grooming sessions. By squeezing both sides of the anus with a soft cloth, you can express some of the material in the sacs. If the material is pasty and thick, you likely will need the assistance of a veterinarian. Vets know how to express the glands and can show you how to do it correctly without hurting the dog or spraying yourself with the unpleasant liquid.

become second nature; he may not like it, but he should at least tolerate it.

Aside from brushing, offer dental toys to your dog and feed crunchy biscuits, which help to minimize plaque. Rope toys have the added benefit of acting like floss as the dog chews. At your adult dog's yearly check-ups, the vet will likely perform a thorough tooth scraping as well as a complete check for any problems. Proper care of your dog's teeth will ensure that you will enjoy your dog's smile for many years to come. The next time your dog goes to give you a hello kiss, you'll be glad you spent the time caring for his teeth.

THE OTHER END

Dogs sometime have trouble with their anal glands, which are sacs located beside the anal vent. These should empty when a dog has normal bowel movements; if they don't, they can become full or impacted, causing discomfort. Owners often are alarmed to see their dogs scooting across the floor, dragging their behinds behind, this is just a dog's attempt to empty the glands himself.

Some brave owners attempt to evacuate their dogs' anal glands themselves during grooming, but no one will tell you that this is a pleasant task! Thus many owners prefer to make the trip to the vet to have the vet take care of the problem; owners whose dogs visit a groomer can have this done by the groomer if he offers this as part of his services. Regardless, don't neglect the dog's other end in your home-care routine. Look for scooting, licking or other signs of discomfort "back there" to ascertain whether the anal glands need to be emptied.

IDENTIFICATION AND TRAVEL

ID FOR YOUR DOG

You love your AWS and want to keep him safe. Of course you take every precaution to prevent his escaping from the yard or becoming lost or stolen. You have a sturdy high fence, and you always keep your dog on lead when out and about in public places. If your dog is not properly identified, however, you are overlooking a major aspect of his safety. We hope to never be in a situation where our dog is missing, but we should practice prevention in the unfortunate case that this happens; identification greatly increases the chances of your dog's being returned to you.

There are several ways to identify your dog. First, the traditional dog tag should be a staple in your dog's wardrobe, attached to his everyday collar. Tags can be made of sturdy

After a long and successful day in the field, it is absolutely necessary to provide your AWS with a safe ride home. Never drive with your AWS unrestrained in your car.

plastic and various metals and should include your contact information so that a person who finds the dog can get in touch with you right away to arrange his return. Many people today enjoy the wide range of decorative tags available, so have fun and create a tag to match your dog's personality. Of course, it is important that the tag stays on the collar, so have a secure "O" ring attachment; you also can explore the type of tag that slides right onto the collar.

In addition to the ID tag, which every dog should wear even if identified by another method, two other forms of identification have become

Identification is essential! A new take on traditional ID tags is a collar with your contact information woven into it to prevent the information from becoming detached from the collar.

popular: microchipping and tattooing. In microchipping, a tiny scannable chip is painlessly inserted under the dog's skin. The number is registered to you so that, if your lost dog turns up at a clinic or shelter, the chip can be scanned to retrieve your contact information.

The advantage of the microchip is that it is a permanent form of ID, but there are some factors to consider. Several different companies make microchips, and not all are compatible with the others' scanning devices. It's best to find a company with a universal microchip that can be read by scanners made by other companies as well. It won't do any good to have the dog chipped if the information cannot be retrieved. Also, not every humane society, shelter and clinic is equipped with a scanner, although more and more

facilities are equipping themselves. In fact, many shelters microchip dogs that they adopt out to new homes.

Because the microchip is not visible to the eye, the dog must wear a tag that states that he is microchipped so that whoever picks him up will know to have him scanned. He of course also should have a tag with your contact information in case his chip cannot be read. Humane societies and veterinary clinics offer this service, which is usually very affordable.

Though less popular than microchipping, tattooing is another permanent method of ID for dogs. Most vets perform this service, and there are also clinics that perform dog tattooing. This is also an affordable procedure and one that will not cause much discomfort for the dog. It is best to put the tattoo in a visible area, such as the ear, to deter theft. It is sad to say that there are cases of dogs' being stolen and sold to research laboratories, but such laboratories will not accept tattooed dogs.

To ensure that the tattoo is effective in aiding your dog's return to you, the tattoo number must be registered with a national organization. That way, when someone finds a tattooed dog a phone call to the registry will quickly match the dog with his owner.

HIT THE ROAD

Car travel with your AWS may be limited to necessity only, such as trips to the vet, or you may bring your dog along almost everywhere you go. This will depend much on your individual dog and how he reacts to rides in the car. You can begin desensitizing your dog to car travel as a pup so that it's something that he's used to. Still, some dogs suffer from motion sickness. Your vet may prescribe a medication for this if trips in the car pose a problem for your dog. At the very least, you will need to get him to the vet, so he will need to tolerate these trips with the least amount of hassle possible.

Start taking your pup on short trips, maybe just around the block to start. If he is fine with short trips, lengthen your rides a little at a time. Start to take him on your errands or just for drives around town. By this time it will be easy to tell whether your dog is a born traveler or would prefer staying at home when you are on the road.

Of course, safety is a concern for dogs in the car. First, he must travel securely, not left loose to roam about the car where he could be injured or distract the driver. A young pup can be held by a passenger initially but should soon graduate to a travel crate, which can be the same crate he uses in the home. Other options include a car harness (like a seat belt for dogs) and partitioning the back of the car with a gate made for this purpose.

Bring along what you will need for the dog. He should wear his collar and ID tags, of course, and you should bring his leash, water (and food if a long trip) and clean-up materials for potty breaks and in case of motion sickness. Always keep your dog on his leash when you make stops, and never leave him alone in the car. Many a dog has died from the heat inside a closed car; this does not take much time at all. A dog left alone inside a car can also be a target for thieves.

UP, UP AND AWAY!

Taking a trip by air does not mean that your dog cannot accompany you, it just means that you will have to be well informed and well prepared. The majority of dogs travel as checked cargo; only the smallest of breeds are allowed in the cabin with their owners. Your dog must travel in an airline-approved travel crate appropriate to his size so that he will be safe and comfortable during the flight. If the crate that you use at home does not meet the airline's specifications, you can purchase one from the airline or from your pet-supply store (making sure it is labeled as airline-approved).

If you are going on vacation and need to board your AWS, research boarding kennels ahead of time. Select a clean kennel with an attentive staff and enough room to allow your AWS daily exercise.

It's best to have the crate in advance of your trip to give the dog time to get accustomed to it. You can put a familiar blanket and a favorite toy or two in the crate with the dog to make him feel at home and to keep him occupied. The crate should be lined with absorbent material for the trip, with bowls for food and water attached to the outside of the crate. The crate must be labeled with your contact information, feeding instructions and a statement asserting that the dog was fed within a certain time frame of arrival at the airport (check with your airline). You will also have to provide proof of current vaccinations.

Again, advance planning is the key to smooth sailing in the skies. Make your reservations well ahead of time and know what restrictions your airline imposes: no travel during certain months, refusal of certain breeds, restrictions on certain destinations, etc. In spite of all of these variables, major carriers have much experience with transporting animals, so have a safe flight.

DOG-FRIENDLY DESTINATIONS
When planning vacations, a question that often arises is, "Who will watch the dog?" More and more families, however, are answering that question with, "We will!" With the rise in dog-friendly places to visit, the number of families who bring their dogs along on vacation is on the rise. A search online for dog-friendly vacation spots will turn up many choices, as well as resources for owners of canine

travelers. Ask others for suggestions: your vet, your breeder,
other dog owners, breed club
members, people at the local
doggie daycare.

Traveling with your American
Water Spaniel means providing
for his comfort and safety, and
you will have to pack a bag for
him just as you do for yourself.
Bring his everyday items: food,
water, bowls, leash and collar
(with ID), brush and comb, toys,
bed, crate plus any additional
accessories that he will need
once you get to your vacation
spot. If he takes medication, don't
forget to bring it with you. If
going camping or on another type
of outdoor excursion, take
precautions to protect your dog
from ticks, mosquitoes and other
pests. Above all, have a good
time with your American Water
Spaniel and enjoy each other's
company.

BOARDING
Today there are many options for
dog owners who need someone to
care for their dogs in certain
circumstances. While many think
of boarding their dogs as
something to do when away on
vacation, many others use the
services of doggie "daycare"
facilities, dropping their dogs off
to spend the day while they are
at work. Many of these facilities
offer both long-term and daily
care. Many go beyond just

boarding and cater to all sorts of
needs, with on-site grooming,
veterinary care, training classes
and even "web-cams" where
owners can log onto the Internet
and check out what their dogs are
up to. Most dogs enjoy the
activity and time spent with
other dogs.

Before you need to use such a
service, check out the ones in
your area. Make visits to see the
facilities, meet the staff, discuss
fees and available services and
see whether this is a place where
you think your dog will be
happy. It is best to do your
research in advance so that
you're not stuck at the last
minute, forced into making a
rushed decision without knowing
whether the kennel that you've
chosen meets your standards.
You also can check with your
vet's office to see whether they
offer boarding for their clients or
can recommend a good kennel in
the area.

The kennel will need to see
proof of your dog's health records
and vaccinations so as not to
spread illness from dog to dog.
Your dog also will need proper
identification. Owners usually
experience some separation
anxiety the first time they have to
leave their dog in someone else's
care, so it's reassuring to know
that the kennel you choose is run
by experienced, caring, true dog
people.

AMERICAN WATER SPANIEL

BASIC TRAINING PRINCIPLES: PUPPY VS. ADULT

There's a big difference between training an adult dog and training a young puppy. With a young puppy, everything is new! At eight to ten weeks of age, he will be experiencing many things, and he has nothing with which to compare these experiences. Up to this point, he has been with his dam and littermates, not one-on-one with people except in his interactions with his breeder and visitors to the litter.

When you first bring the puppy home, he is eager to please you. This means that he accepts doing things your way. During the next couple of months, he will absorb the basis of everything he needs to know for the rest of his life. This early age is even referred to as the "sponge" stage. After that, for the next 18 months, it's up to you to reinforce good manners by building on the foundation that you've established. Once your puppy is reliable in basic commands and behavior and has reached the appropriate age, you may gradually introduce him to some of the interesting sports, games and activities available to pet owners and their dogs.

Raising your puppy is a family affair. Each member of the family must know what rules to set forth for the puppy and how to use the same one-word commands to mean exactly the same thing every time. Even if yours is a large family, one person will soon be considered by the pup to be the leader, the alpha person in his pack, the "boss" who must be obeyed. Often that highly regarded person turns out to be the one who feeds the puppy. Food ranks very high on the puppy's list of important

Here's a young American Water Spaniel sponge, waiting to soak up whatever you teach him. Douse him now when he is still young.

things! That's why your puppy is rewarded with small treats along with verbal praise when he responds to you correctly. As the puppy learns to do what you want him to do, the food rewards are gradually eliminated and only the praise remains. If you were to keep up with the food treats, you could have two problems on your hands—an obese dog and a beggar.

Training begins the minute your AWS puppy steps through the doorway of your home, so don't make the mistake of putting the puppy on the floor and telling him by your actions to "Go for it! Run wild!" Even if this is your first puppy, you must act as if you know what you're doing: be the boss. An uncertain pup may be

OUR CANINE KIDS

"Everything I learned about parenting, I learned from my dog." How often adults recognize that their parenting skills are mere extensions of the education they acquired while caring for their dogs. Many owners refer to their dogs as their "kids" and treat their canine companions like real members of the family. Surveys indicate that a majority of dog owners talk to their dogs regularly, celebrate their dogs' birthdays and purchase Christmas gifts for their dogs. Another survey shows that dog owners take their dogs to the veterinarian more frequently than they visit their own physicians.

terrified to move, while a bold one will be ready to take you at your word and start plotting to destroy the house! Before you collected your puppy, you decided where his own special place would be, and that's where to put him when you first arrive home. Give him a house tour after he has investigated his area and had a nap and a bathroom "pit stop."

It's worth mentioning here that if you've adopted an adult dog that is completely trained to

An attentive puppy is the best student. Never train your puppy in an area where there are many distractions.

DAILY SCHEDULE
How many relief trips does your puppy need per day? A puppy up to the age of 14 weeks will need to go outside about 8 to 12 times per day! You will have to take the pup out any time he starts sniffing around the floor or turning in small circles, as well as after naps, meals, games and lessons or whenever he's released from his crate. Once the puppy is 14 to 22 weeks of age, he will require only 6 to 8 relief trips. At the ages of 22 to 32 weeks, the puppy will require about 5 to 7 trips. Adult dogs typically require 4 relief trips per day, in the morning, afternoon, evening and late at night.

impossible for the dog to accept. After all, he's been successful so far by doing everything his way. (Patience again.) He may agree with your instruction for a few days and then slip back into his old ways, so you must be just as consistent and understanding in your teaching as you would be with a puppy. (More patience needed yet again.) Your dog has to learn to pay attention to your voice, your family, the daily routine, new smells, new sounds and, in some cases, even a new climate.

One of the most important things to find out about a newly adopted adult dog is his reaction to children (yours and others), strangers and your friends and how he acts upon meeting other dogs. If he was not socialized with dogs as a puppy, this could be a major problem. This does not mean that he's a "bad" dog, a vicious dog or an aggressive dog; rather, it means that he has no idea how to read another dog's body language. There's no way for him to tell whether the other dog is a friend or foe. Survival instinct takes over, telling him to attack first and ask questions later. This definitely calls for professional help and, even then, may not be a behavior that can be corrected 100% reliably (or even at all). If you have a puppy, this is why it is so very important to introduce your young puppy

your liking, lucky you! You're off the hook! However, if that dog spent his life up to this point in a kennel, or even in a good home but without any real training, be prepared to tackle the job ahead. A dog three years of age or older with no previous training cannot be blamed for not knowing what he was never taught. While the dog is trying to understand and learn your rules, at the same time he has to unlearn many of his previously self-taught habits and general view of the world.

Working with a professional trainer will speed up your progress with an adopted adult dog. You'll need patience, too. Some new rules may be close to properly to other puppies and "dog-friendly" adult dogs.

HOUSE-TRAINING YOUR AWS

Dogs are tactility-oriented when it comes to house-training. In other words, they respond to the surface on which they are given approval to eliminate. The choice is yours (the dog's version is in parentheses): The lawn (including the neighbors' lawns)? A bare patch of earth under a tree (where people like to sit and relax in the summertime)? Concrete steps or patio (all sidewalks, garages and basement floors)? The curbside (watch out for cars)? A small area of crushed stone in a corner of the yard (mine!)? The latter is the best choice if you can manage it, because it will remain strictly for the dog's use and is easy to keep clean.

You can start out with paper-training indoors and switch over to an outdoor surface as the puppy matures and gains control over his need to eliminate. For the naysayers, don't worry—this won't mean that the dog will soil on every piece of newspaper lying around the house. You are training him to go outside, remember? Starting out by paper-training often is the only choice for a city dog.

WHEN YOUR PUPPY'S "GOT TO GO"

Your puppy's need to relieve himself is seemingly non-stop,

but signs of improvement will be seen each week. From 8 to 10 weeks old, the puppy will have to be taken outside every time he wakes up, about 10–15 minutes after every meal and after every period of play—all day long, from first thing in the morning until his bedtime! That's a total of ten or more trips per day to teach the puppy where it's okay to relieve himself. With that schedule in mind, you can see that house-training a young puppy is not a part-time job. It requires someone to be home all day.

If that seems overwhelming or impossible, do a little planning. For example, plan to pick up your puppy at the start of a vacation period. If you can't get home in the middle of the day,

Consistency is the key to making good potty habits just another part of the daily routine.

Baby gates can be used to confine your AWS in an area in the house you deem safe when you don't want him to have free range of the home.

An "ex-pen," sturdy enough that the pup can't knock it over, is a helpful tool in confining your pup. This type of pen is portable and easily assembled.

Likewise, it's a busy family area that will accustom the pup to a variety of noises, everything from pots and pans to the telephone, blender and dishwasher. He will also be enchanted by the smell of your cooking (and will never be critical when you burn something). An exercise pen (also called an "ex-pen," a puppy version of a playpen) within the room of choice is an excellent means of confinement for a young pup. He can see out and has a certain amount of space in which to run about, but he is safe from dangerous things like electrical cords, heating units, trash baskets or open kitchen-supply cabinets. Place the pen where the puppy will not get a blast of heat or air conditioning.

In the pen, you can put a few toys, his bed (which can be his crate if the dimensions of pen and crate are compatible) and a few layers of newspaper in one

plan to hire a dog-sitter or ask a neighbor to come over to take the pup outside, feed him his lunch and then take him out again about ten or so minutes after he's eaten. Also make arrangements with that or another person to be your "emergency" contact if you have to stay late on the job. Remind yourself—repeatedly— that this hectic schedule improves as the puppy gets older.

HOME WITHIN A HOME
Your AWS puppy needs to be confined to one secure, puppy-proof area when no one is able to watch his every move. Generally the kitchen is the place of choice because the floor is washable.

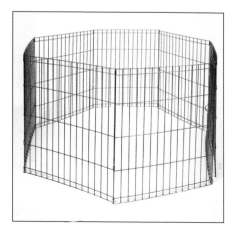

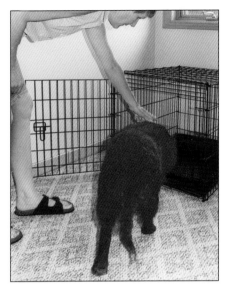

small corner, just in case. A water bowl can be hung at a convenient height on the side of the ex-pen so it won't become a splashing pool for an innovative puppy. His food dish can go on the floor, next to but not under the water bowl.

Crates are something that pet owners are at last getting used to for their dogs. Wild or domestic canines have always preferred to sleep in den-like safe spots, and that is exactly what the crate provides. How often have you seen adult dogs that choose to sleep under a table or chair even though they have full run of the house? It's the den connection.

In your "happy" voice, use the word "Crate" every time you put the pup into his den. If he's new to a crate, toss in a small biscuit for him to chase the first

The benefits of crate-training are many and when your AWS is introduced to it properly, he will go there when told without any fuss—and enjoy his "den."

few times. At night, after he's been outside, he should sleep in his crate. The crate may be kept in his designated area at night or, if you want to be sure to hear those wake-up yips in the morning, put the crate in a corner of your bedroom. However, don't make any response whatsoever to whining or crying. If he's

EXTRA! EXTRA!

The headlines read: "Puppy Piddles Here!" Breeders commonly use newspapers to line their whelping pens, so puppies learn to associate newspapers with relieving themselves. Do not use newspapers to line your pup's crate, as this will signal to your puppy that it is OK to urinate in his crate. If you choose to paper-train your puppy, you will layer newspapers on a section of the floor near the door he uses to go outside. You should encourage the puppy to use the papers to relieve himself, and bring him there whenever you see him getting ready to go. Little by little, you will reduce the size of the newspaper-covered area so that the puppy will learn to relieve himself "on the other side of the door."

completely ignored, he'll settle down and get to sleep.

Good bedding for a young puppy is an old folded bath towel or an old blanket, something that is easily washable and disposable if necessary ("accidents" will happen!). Never put newspaper in the puppy's crate. Also those old ideas about adding a clock to replace his mother's heartbeat or a hot-water bottle to replace her warmth, are just that—old ideas. The clock could drive the puppy nuts, and the hot-water bottle could end up as a very soggy waterbed. An extremely good breeder would have introduced your puppy to the crate by letting two pups sleep together for a couple of nights, followed by several nights alone. How thankful you will be if you found that breeder!

Safe toys in the pup's crate or area will keep him occupied, but monitor their condition closely. Discard any toys that show signs of being chewed to bits. Squeaky parts, bits of stuffing or plastic or any other small pieces can cause intestinal blockage or possibly choking if ingested.

PROGRESSING WITH POTTY-TRAINING

After you've taken your puppy out and he has relieved himself in the area you've selected, he can have some free time with the family as long as there is someone responsible for watching him. That doesn't mean just someone in the same room who is watching TV or busy on the computer but one person who is doing nothing other than keeping an eye on the pup, playing with him on the floor and helping him understand his position in the pack.

This first taste of freedom will let you begin to set the house rules. If you don't want the dog on the furniture, now is the time to prevent his first attempts to jump up onto the couch. The word to use in this case is "Off," not "Down." "Down" is the word you will use to teach the down position, which is something entirely different.

Most corrections at this stage come in the form of simply distracting the puppy. Instead of telling him "No" for "Don't chew the carpet," distract the chomping puppy with a toy and he'll forget about the carpet.

As you are playing with the pup, do not forget to watch him closely and pay attention to his body language. Whenever you see him begin to circle or sniff, take the puppy outside to relieve himself. If you are paper-training, put him back into his confined area on the newspapers. In either case, praise him as he eliminates while he actually is in the act of relieving himself. Three seconds after he has finished is too late! You'll be praising him for

running toward you, picking up a toy or whatever he may be doing at that moment, and that's not what you want to be praising him for. Timing is a vital tool in all dog training. Use it.

Remove soiled newspapers immediately and replace them with clean ones. You may want to take a small piece of soiled paper and place it in the middle of the new clean papers, as the scent will attract him to that spot when it's time to go again. That scent attraction is why it's so important to clean up any messes made in the house by using a product specially made to eliminate the odor of dog urine and droppings. Regular household cleansers won't do the trick. Pet shops sell the best pet deodorizers. Invest in the largest container you can find.

You select the area in which your AWS is to relieve himself. Once trained, he will always return to the same spot—regardless of the current weather conditions.

Scent attraction eventually will lead your pup to his chosen spot outdoors; this is the basis of outdoor training. When you take your puppy outside to relieve himself, use a one-word command such as "Outside" or "Go-potty" (that's one word to the puppy) as you attach his leash. Then quickly lead him to his spot. Now comes the hard part—hard for you, that is. Just stand there until he urinates and defecates. Move him a few feet in one direction or another if he's just sitting there looking at you, but remember that this is neither playtime nor time for a walk. This is strictly a business trip. Then, as he circles and squats (remember your timing), give him a quiet "Good dog" as praise. If you start to jump for joy, ecstatic over his performance, he'll do one of two things: either he will stop mid-stream, as it were, or he'll do it again for you—in the house—and expect you to be just as delighted!

Give him five minutes or so and, if he doesn't go in that time, take him back indoors to his confined area and try again in another ten minutes or immediately if you see him sniffing and circling. By careful observation, you'll soon work out a successful schedule.

Accidents, by the way, are just that—accidents. Clean them up quickly and thoroughly, without comment, after the puppy has been taken outside to finish his business and then put back into his area or crate. If you witness an accident in progress, say "No!" in a stern voice and get the pup outdoors immediately. No punishment is needed. You and your puppy are just learning each other's language, and sometimes it's easy to miss a puppy's message. Chalk it up to experience and watch more closely from now on.

KEEPING THE PACK ORDERLY
Discipline is a form of training that brings order to life. For example, military discipline is what allows the soldiers in an army to work as one. Discipline is a form of teaching and, in dogs, is the basis of how the successful pack operates. Each member knows his place in the pack and all respect the leader, or alpha dog. It is essential for your puppy that you establish this type of relationship, with you as the alpha, or leader. It is a form of social coexistence that all canines recognize and accept. Discipline, therefore, is never to be confused with punishment. When you teach your puppy how you want him to behave, and he behaves properly and you praise him for it, you are disciplining him with a form of positive reinforcement.

For a dog, rewards come in the form of praise, a smile, a

cheerful tone of voice, a few friendly pats or a rub of the ears. Rewards are also small food treats. Obviously, that does not mean bits of regular dog food. Instead, treats are very small bits of special things like cheese or pieces of soft dog treats. The idea is to reward the dog with something very small that he can taste and swallow, providing instant positive reinforcement. If he has to take time to chew the treat, by the time he is finished he will have forgotten what he did to earn it!

Your puppy should never be physically punished. The displeasure shown on your face and in your voice is sufficient to signal to the pup that he has done something wrong. He wants to please everyone higher up on the social ladder, especially his leader, so a scowl and harsh voice will take care of the error. Growling out the word "Shame!" when the pup is caught in the act of doing something wrong is better than the repetitive "No." Some dogs hear "No" so often that they begin to think it's their name! By the way, do not use the dog's name when you're correcting him. His name is reserved to get his attention for something pleasant about to take place.

There are punishments that have nothing to do with you. For example, your dog may think that chasing cats is one reason for his existence. You can try to stop it as much as you like but without success, because it's such fun for the dog. But one good hissing, spitting swipe of a cat's claws across the dog's nose will put an end to the game forever. Intervene only when your dog's eyeball is seriously at risk. Cat scratches can cause permanent damage to an innocent but annoying puppy.

PUPPY KINDERGARTEN

COLLAR AND LEASH
Before you begin your AWS puppy's education, he must be used to his collar and leash. Choose a collar for your puppy that is secure but not heavy or bulky. He won't enjoy training if he's uncomfortable. A flat buckle collar is fine for everyday wear

Your AWS must be used to and comfortable with his leash before you can begin training.

and for initial puppy training. For older dogs, there are several types of training collars such as the martingale, which is a double loop that tightens slightly around the neck, or the head collar, which is similar to a horse's halter. Do not use a chain choke collar unless you have been specifically shown how to put it on and how to use it. You may not be disposed to use a chain choke collar even if your breeder has told you that it's suitable for your AWS.

A lightweight 6-foot woven cotton or nylon training leash is preferred by most trainers because it is easy to fold up in your hand and comfortable to hold because there is a certain amount of give to it. There are lessons where the dog will start off 6 feet away from you at the end of the leash. The leash used to take the puppy outside to relieve himself is shorter because you don't want him to roam away from his area. The shorter leash will also be the one to use when you walk the puppy.

If you've been wise enough to enroll in a puppy kindergarten training class, suggestions will be made as to the best collar and leash for your young puppy. I say "wise" because your puppy will be in a class with puppies in his age range (up to five months old) of all breeds and sizes. It's the perfect way for him to learn the right way (and the wrong way) to interact with other dogs as well as their people. You cannot teach

Your American Water Spaniel's instinctive traits must be taken into account when undertaking training.

your puppy how to interpret another dog's sign language. For a first-time puppy owner, these socialization classes are invaluable. For experienced dog owners, they are a real boon to further training.

ATTENTION
You've been using the dog's name since the minute you collected him from the breeder, so you should be able to get his attention by saying his name—with a big smile and in an excited tone of voice. His response will be the puppy equivalent of "Here I am! What are we going to do?" Your

immediate response (if you haven't guessed by now) is "Good dog." Rewarding him at the moment he pays attention to you teaches him the proper way to respond when he hears his name.

For a sporting breed who will be working with you off leash in the field, your AWS must be absolutely reliable in the basic commands.

EXERCISES FOR A BASIC CANINE EDUCATION

THE SIT EXERCISE
There are several ways to teach the puppy to sit. The first one is to catch him whenever he is about to sit and, as his backside nears the floor, say "Sit, good dog!" That's positive reinforcement and, if your timing is sharp, he will learn that what he's doing at that second is connected to your saying "Sit" and that you think he's clever for doing it!

Another method is to start

DON'T STRESS ME OUT
Your dog doesn't have to deal with paying the bills, the daily commute, PTA meetings and the like, but, believe it or not, there's a lot of stress in a dog's world. Stress can be caused by the owner's impatient demeanor and his angry or harsh corrections. If your dog cringes when you reach for his training collar, he's stressed. An older dog is sometimes stressed out when he goes to a new home. No matter what the cause, put off all training until he's over it. If he's going through a fear period—shying away from people, trembling when spoken to, avoiding eye contact or hiding under furniture—wait to resume training. Naturally you'd also postpone your lessons if the dog were sick, and the same goes for you. Show some compassion.

with the puppy on his leash in front of you. Show him a treat in the palm of your right hand. Bring your hand up under his nose and, almost in slow motion, move your hand up and back so his nose goes up in the air and his head tilts back as he follows the treat in your hand. At that point, he will have to either sit or fall over, so as his back legs buckle under, say "Sit, good dog," and then give him the treat and lots of praise. You may have to begin with your hand lightly running up his chest, actually lifting his chin up until he sits. Some (usually older) dogs require gentle pressure on their hindquarters with the left hand, in which case the dog should be on your left side. Puppies generally do not appreciate this physical dominance.

After a few times, you should be able to show the dog a treat in the open palm of your hand, raise your hand waist-high as you say "Sit" and have him sit. You will thereby have taught him two things at the same time. Both the verbal command and the motion of the hand are signals for the sit. Your puppy is watching you almost more than he is listening to you, so what you do is just as important as what you say.

Don't save any of these drills only for training sessions. Use them as much as possible at odd times during a normal day. The dog should always sit before being given his food dish. He should sit to let you go through a doorway first, when the doorbell rings or when you stop to speak to someone on the street.

A SIMPLE "SIT"

When you command your dog to sit, use the word "Sit." Do not say "Sit down," as your dog will not know whether you mean "Sit" or "Down," or maybe you mean both. Be clear in your instructions to your dog; use one-word commands and always be consistent.

THE DOWN EXERCISE

Before beginning to teach the down command, you must consider how the dog feels about this exercise. To him, "down" is a submissive position. Being flat on the floor with you standing over him is not his idea of fun. It's up to you to let him know that, while it may not be fun, the reward of your approval is worth his effort.

Start with the puppy on your left side in a sit position. Hold the leash right above his collar in your left hand. Have an extra-special treat, such as a small piece of cooked chicken or hot dog, in your right hand. Place it at the end of the pup's nose and steadily move your hand down and forward along the ground. Hold the leash to prevent a sudden lunge for the food. As the puppy goes into the down position, say "Down" very gently.

The difficulty with this exercise is twofold: it's both the submissive aspect and the fact that most people say the word "Down" as if they were a drill sergeants in charge of recruits! So issue the command sweetly, give him the treat and have the pup maintain the down position for several seconds. If he tries to get up immediately, place your hands on his shoulders and press down gently, giving him a very quiet "Good dog." As you progress with this lesson, increase the "down

time" until he will hold it until you say "Okay" (his cue for release). Practice this one in the house at various times throughout the day.

By increasing the length of time during which the dog must maintain the down position, you'll find many uses for it. For example, he can lie at your feet in the vet's office or anywhere that

DOWN

"Down" is a harsh-sounding word and a submissive posture in dog body language, thus presenting two obstacles in teaching the down command. When the dog is about to flop down on his own, tell him "Good down." Pups that are not good about being handled learn better by having food lowered in front of them. A dog that trusts you can be gently guided into position. When you give the command "Down," be sure to say it sweetly!

Always introduce new lessons with the dog on lead. Here, an AWS and his owner practice the sit/stay.

your left hand, and let the dog know that you have a treat in your closed right hand. Step forward on your right foot as you say "Stay." Immediately turn and stand directly in front of the dog, keeping your right hand up high so he'll keep his eye on the treat hand and maintain the sit position for a count of five. Return to your original position and offer the reward.

Increase the length of the sit/stay each time until the dog can hold it for at least 30 seconds without moving. After about a week of success, move out on your right foot and take two steps before turning to face the dog. Give the "Stay" hand signal (left palm back toward the dog's head) as you leave. He gets the treat when you return and he holds the sit/stay. Increase the distance that you walk away from him before turning until you reach the length of your training leash. But don't rush it. Go back to the beginning if he moves before he should. No matter what the lesson, never be upset by having to back up for a few days. The repetition and practice are what will make your dog reliable in these commands. It won't do any good to move on to something more difficult if the command is not mastered at the easier levels. Above all, even if you do get frustrated, never let your puppy know! Always keep a positive, upbeat attitude during

both of you have to wait, when you are on the phone, while the family is eating and so forth. If you progress to training for competitive obedience, he'll already be all set for the exercise called the "long down."

THE STAY EXERCISE

You can teach your AWS to stay in the sit, down and stand positions. To teach the sit/stay, have the dog sit on your left side. Hold the leash at waist level in training, which will transmit to your dog for positive results.

The down/stay is taught in the same way once the dog is completely reliable and steady with the down command. Again, don't rush it. With the dog in the down position on your left side, step out on your right foot as you say "Stay." Return by walking around in back of the dog and into your original position. While you are training, it's okay to murmur something like "Hold on" to encourage him to stay put. When the dog will stay without moving when you are at a distance of 3 or 4 feet, begin to increase the length of time before you return. Be sure he holds the down on your return until you say "Okay." At that point, he gets his treat—just so he'll remember for next time that it's not over until it's over.

THE COME EXERCISE

No command is more important to the safety of your American Water Spaniel than "Come." It is what you should say every single time you see the puppy running toward you: "Dylan, come! Good dog." During playtime, run a few feet away from the puppy and turn and tell him to "Come" as he is already running to you. You can go so far as to teach your puppy two things at once if you squat down and hold out your arms. As the pup gets close to you and you're saying "Good dog," bring your right arm in about waist-high. Now he's also learning the hand signal, an excellent device should you be on the phone when you need to get him to come to you. You'll also both be one step ahead when you enter obedience classes.

You want your AWS to come enthusiastically when he hears his name, especially when he is working in the field.

When the puppy responds to your well-timed "Come," try it with the puppy on the training leash. This time, catch him off guard, while he's sniffing a leaf or watching a bird: "Dylan, come!" You may have to pause for a split second after his name to be sure you have his attention. If the puppy shows any sign of confusion, give the leash a mild jerk and take a couple of steps backward. Do not repeat the command. In this case, you should say "Good come" as he reaches you.

That's the number-one rule of training. Each command word is given just once. Anything more is nagging. You'll also notice that all commands are one word only. Even when they are actually two words, you say them as one.

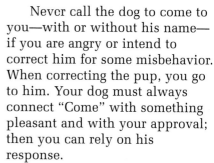

Never call the dog to come to you—with or without his name—if you are angry or intend to correct him for some misbehavior. When correcting the pup, you go to him. Your dog must always connect "Come" with something pleasant and with your approval; then you can rely on his response.

Puppies, like children, have notoriously short attention spans, so don't overdo it with any of the training. Keep each lesson short. Break it up with a quick run around the yard or a ball toss, repeat the lesson and quit as soon as the pup gets it right. That way, you will always end with a "Good dog."

Life isn't perfect and neither are puppies. A time will come, often around ten months of age, when he'll become "selectively deaf" or choose to "forget" his name. He may respond by wagging his tail (and even seeming to smile at you) with a look that says "Make me!" Laugh, throw his favorite toy and skip the lesson you had planned. Pups will be pups!

THE HEEL EXERCISE

The second most important command to teach, after the come, is the heel. When you are walking your growing puppy, you need to be in control. Besides, it looks terrible to be pulled and yanked down the street, and it's

STAY OF EXECUTION

To begin, step away from the dog, who is in the sit position, on your right foot. That tells the dog you aren't going anywhere. Turn and stand directly in front of him so he won't be tempted to follow. Two seconds is a long, long time to your dog, so increase the time for which he's expected to stay only in short increments. Don't force it. When practicing the heel exercise, your dog will sit at your side whenever you stop. Don't stop for more than three seconds, as your enthusiastic dog will really feel that it's an eternity!

not much fun either. Your eight-to ten-week-old puppy will probably follow you everywhere, but that's his natural instinct, not your control over the situation. However, any time he does follow you, you can say "Heel" and be ahead of the game, as he will learn to associate this command with the action of following you before you even begin teaching him to heel.

There is a very precise, almost military, procedure for teaching your dog to heel. As with all other obedience training, begin with the dog on your left side. He will be in a very nice sit and you will have the training leash across your chest. Hold the loop and folded leash in your right hand. Pick up the slack leash above the dog in your left hand and hold it loosely at your side. Step out on your left foot as you say "Heel." If the puppy does not move, give a gentle tug or pat your left leg to get him started. If he surges ahead of you, stop and pull him back gently until he is at your side. Tell him to sit and begin again.

Walk a few steps and stop while the puppy is correctly beside you. Tell him to sit and give mild verbal praise. (More enthusiastic praise will encourage him to think the lesson is over.) Repeat the lesson, increasing the number of steps you take only as long as the dog is heeling nicely

beside you. When you end the lesson, have him hold the sit, then give him the "Okay" to let him know that this is the end of the lesson. Praise him so that he knows he did a good job.

The cure for excessive pulling (a common problem) is to stop when the dog is no more than 2 or 3 feet ahead of you. Guide him back into position and begin again. With a really determined puller, try switching to a head collar. This will automatically turn the pup's head toward you so you can bring him back easily

Heeling means that the dog walks next to you at the pace that you set, not the other way around.

to the heel position. Give quiet, reassuring praise every time the leash goes slack and he's staying with you.

Staying and heeling can take a lot out of a dog, so provide playtime and free-running exercise to shake off the stress when the lessons are over. You don't want him to associate training with all work and no fun.

TAPERING OFF TIDBITS
Your dog has been watching you—and the hand that treats—throughout all of his lessons, and now it's time to break the treat habit. Begin by giving him treats at the end of each lesson only. Then start to give a treat after the end of only some of the lessons.

As you progress with your AWS's training, you will use treats more sparingly, but never skimp on the praise.

At the end of every lesson, as well as during the lessons, be consistent with the praise. Your pup now doesn't know whether he'll get a treat or not, but he should keep performing well just in case! Finally, you will stop giving treat rewards entirely. Save them for something brand-new that you want to teach him. Keep up the praise and you'll always have a "good dog."

OBEDIENCE CLASSES
The advantages of an obedience class are that your dog will have to learn amid the distractions of other people and dogs and that your mistakes will be quickly corrected by the trainer. Teaching your dog along with a qualified instructor and other handlers who may have more dog experience than you is another plus of the class environment. The instructor and other handlers can help you to find the most efficient way of teaching your dog a command or exercise. It's often easier to learn from other people's mistakes than from your own. You will also learn all of the requirements for competitive obedience trials, in which you can earn titles and go on to advanced jumping and retrieving exercises, which are fun for many dogs. Obedience classes build the foundation needed for many other canine activities (in which we humans are allowed to participate, too!).

TRAINING FOR WATER SPORTS

American Water Spaniels love the water, but they need to be introduced to it sensibly. Puppies will play at the edge of a lake or stream, like a small child at the beach. They will stick their noses in it, take a few laps, slap at it and try to get a stone they see at the bottom. They might even try to dig. Some may step right in and swim, but not all. For those daring pups that start right out swimming, remember they are using some muscles in a way they usually do not. They are pulling against water. Just throw a small bumper or a ball a bit beyond their reach, and let your pup have the pleasure of getting it. Later on you can increase the distance, but with a puppy, keep it very short.

For those pups that don't jump right in but are content to play at the edge, let them investigate the shore and edge of the water. Let them have their fun. Never force them or toss them in. That could frighten a pup as it would a small child. Even if you take the pup with older dogs that are retrieving bumpers or balls, he may not be interested. He may just want to explore, so let him. Eventually he will swim.

After a few trips to calm water, toss a bumper a couple of feet out where the pup can get it without swimming. Praise him when he picks it up. Do this a few times on the first day. After that,

gradually put it out just far enough so that he has to step out but can still feel the bottom. Little by little, put it where he has to paddle a few strokes to get it. Now he is building confidence and enjoying the success of getting the bumper. Once he seems happy with the game, you can increase the distance, but with a puppy, keep it close. He hasn't built up his swimming muscles yet.

At the seashore where there are waves, you may find it takes a bit longer. Picture how big a wave must look from the pup's height.

Don't forget to keep hunting fun and enjoyable for your AWS student. He has to love his job in the field.

One of the most natural activities for an AWS to learn is retrieving in water.

Again, let him play and chase the waves as you supervise. He will run back to safety. Later on you can step in yourself, holding him as you would a small child. He will cling to you. You can let him see how you are enjoying it. You can hold a hand under him and let him "swim." Do this for a while, then go close to shore, let him go and give him a gentle push toward the shore. He will set out for shore, but the main thing is not to rush him. He will eventually love swimming with you once he discovers the joy of having you throw bumpers, and he will want you to play, not sit in a beach chair and read. He will never get tired and will keep dropping the wet thing in your lap.

Swimming with your older

dogs is fun but be careful, as their nails will rake you. They may swim in circles around you, almost sinking you. They seem to feel you are in danger and are trying to help you.

At the beginning of swimming season, just remember that the dog hasn't been using those certain muscles for a while. Like any athlete starting training, sessions should be short at first, gradually working up to longer ones.

TRAINING FOR OTHER ACTIVITIES

Once your dog has basic obedience under his collar and is 12 months of age, you can enter the world of agility training. Dogs think agility is pure fun, like being turned loose in an amusement park full of

With his webbed feet, the AWS is a strong swimmer, making water-retrieves a piece of cake.

When the element of surprise is essential in the hunt, the low-profile AWS can't be beat.

obstacles! In addition to agility, there are hunting activities for sporting dogs, lure-coursing events for sighthounds, go-to-ground events for terriers, racing for the Nordic sled dogs, herding trials for the shepherd breeds and tracking, which is open to all "nosey" dogs (which would include all dogs!). For those who like to volunteer, there is the wonderful feeling of owning a therapy dog and visiting hospices, nursing homes and veterans' homes to bring smiles, comfort and companion-

ship to those who live there.

Around the house, your AWS can be taught to do some simple chores. You might teach him to carry a basket of household items or to fetch the morning newspaper. The kids can teach the dog all kinds of tricks, from playing hide-and-seek to balancing a biscuit on his nose. A family dog is what rounds out the family. Everything he does, including sitting in your lap or gazing lovingly at you, represents the bonus of owning a dog.

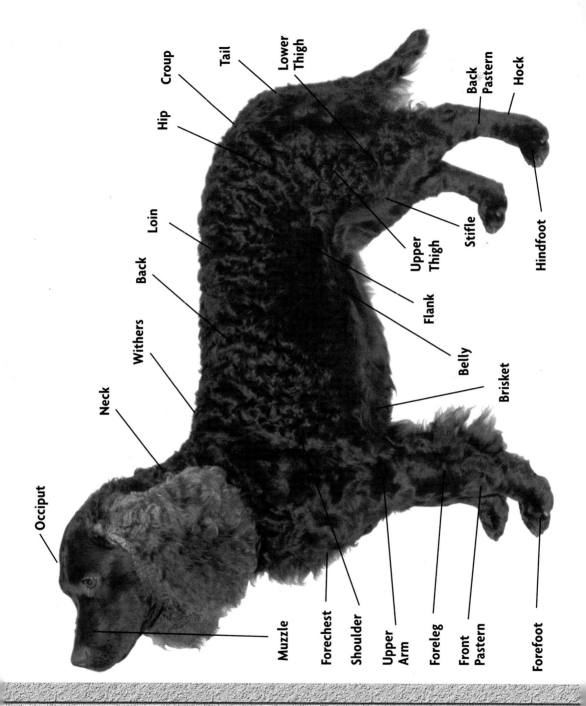

Occiput

Neck

Withers

Back

Loin

Hip

Croup

Tail

Lower Thigh

Back Pastern

Hock

Hindfoot

Stifle

Upper Thigh

Flank

Belly

Brisket

Muzzle

Forechest

Shoulder

Upper Arm

Foreleg

Front Pastern

Forefoot

PHYSICAL STRUCTURE OF THE AMERICAN WATER SPANIEL

HEALTHCARE OF YOUR

AMERICAN WATER SPANIEL

By Lowell Ackerman DVM, DACVD

HEALTHCARE FOR A LIFETIME

When you own a dog, you become his healthcare advocate over his entire lifespan, as well as being the one to shoulder the financial burden of such care. Accordingly, it is worthwhile to focus on prevention rather than treatment, as you and your pet will both be happier.

Of course, the best place to have begun your program of preventive healthcare is with the initial purchase or adoption of your dog. There is no way of guaranteeing that your new furry friend is free of medical problems, but there are some things you can do to improve your odds. You certainly should have done adequate research into the American Water Spaniel and have selected your puppy carefully rather than buying on impulse. Health issues aside, a large number of pet abandonment and relinquishment cases arise from a mismatch between pet needs and owner expectations. This is entirely preventable with appropriate planning and finding a good breeder.

Regarding healthcare issues specifically, it is very difficult to make blanket statements about where to acquire a problem-free pet, but, again, a reputable breeder is your best bet. In an ideal situation you have the opportunity to see both parents, get references from other owners of the breeder's pups and see genetic-testing documentation for several generations of the litter's ancestors. At the very least, you must thoroughly investigate the American Water Spaniel and the problems inherent in that breed, as well as the genetic testing available to screen for those problems. Genetic testing offers some important benefits, but testing is available for only a few disorders in a relatively small number of breeds and is not available for some of the most common genetic diseases, such as hip dysplasia, cataracts, epilepsy, cardiomyopathy, etc. This area of research is indeed exciting and increasingly important, and advances will continue to be made each year. In fact, recent research has shown that there is an equivalent dog gene for 75% of known human genes, so research done in either species is likely to benefit the other.

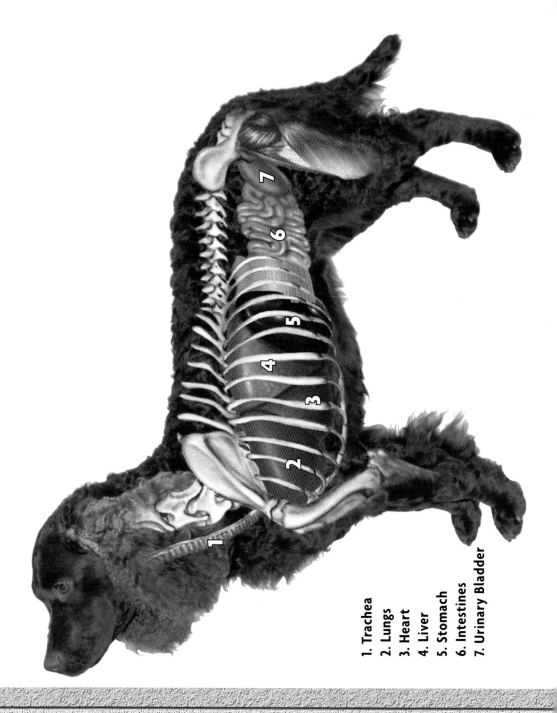

1. Trachea
2. Lungs
3. Heart
4. Liver
5. Stomach
6. Intestines
7. Urinary Bladder

INTERNAL ORGANS OF THE AMERICAN WATER SPANIEL

We've also discussed that evaluating the behavioral nature of your AWS and that of his immediate family members is an important part of the selection process that cannot be overemphasized. It is sometimes difficult to evaluate temperament in puppies because certain behavioral tendencies, such as some forms of aggression, may not be immediately evident. More dogs are euthanized each year for behavioral reasons than for all medical conditions combined, so it is critical to take temperament issues seriously. Start with a well-balanced, friendly companion and put the time and effort into proper socialization, and you will both be rewarded with a lifelong valued relationship.

Assuming that you have started off with a pup from healthy, sound stock, you then become responsible for helping your veterinarian keep your pet healthy. Some crucial things happen before you even bring your puppy home. Parasite control typically begins at two weeks of age, and vaccinations typically begin at six to eight weeks of age. A prepubertal evaluation is typically scheduled for about six months of age. At this time, a dental evaluation is done (since the adult teeth are now in), heartworm prevention is started and neutering or spaying is most commonly done.

It is critical to commence regular dental care at home if you have not already done so. It may not sound very important, but most dogs have active periodontal disease by four years of age if they don't have their teeth cleaned regularly at home, not just at their veterinary exams. Dental problems lead to more than just bad "doggy breath." Gum disease can have very serious medical consequences. If you start brushing your dog's teeth and using antiseptic rinses from a young age, your dog will be accustomed to it and will not resist. The results will be healthy dentition, which your pet will need to enjoy a long, healthy life.

Most dogs are considered adults at a year of age, although some larger breeds still have some filling out to do up to about two or so years old. Even individual dogs within each breed have different healthcare requirements, so work with your veterinarian to determine what will be needed and what your role should be. This doctor-client relationship is important, because as vaccination guidelines change, there may not be an annual "vaccine visit" scheduled. You must make sure that you see your veterinarian at least annually, even if no vaccines are due, because this is the best opportunity to coordinate healthcare activities and to make sure that no medical issues creep by unaddressed.

When your AWS reaches three-quarters of his anticipated lifespan, he is considered a "senior" and likely requires some special care. In

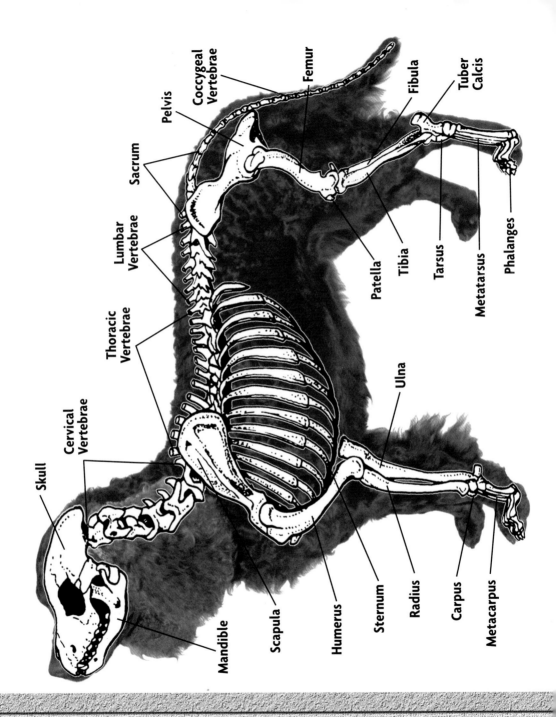

Coccygeal Vertebrae
Femur
Fibula
Tuber Calcis
Pelvis
Sacrum
Lumbar Vertebrae
Patella
Tibia
Tarsus
Metatarsus
Phalanges
Thoracic Vertebrae
Cervical Vertebrae
Skull
Ulna
Mandible
Scapula
Humerus
Sternum
Radius
Carpus
Metacarpus

SKELETAL STRUCTURE OF THE AMERICAN WATER SPANIEL

general, if you've been taking great care of your canine companion throughout his formative and adult years, the transition to senior status should be a smooth one. Age is not a disease, and as long as everything is functioning as it should, there is no reason why most of late adulthood should not be rewarding for both you and your pet. This is especially true if you have tended to the details, such as regular veterinary visits, proper dental care, excellent nutrition and management of bone and joint issues.

At this stage in your AWS's life, your veterinarian may want to schedule visits twice yearly, instead of once, to run some laboratory screenings, electrocardiograms and the like, and to change the diet to something more digestible. Catching problems early is the best way to manage them effectively. Treating the early stages of heart disease is so much easier than trying to intervene when there is more significant damage to the heart muscle. Similarly, managing the beginning of kidney problems is fairly routine if there is no significant kidney damage. Other problems, like cognitive dysfunction (similar to senility and Alzheimer's disease), cancer, diabetes and arthritis, are more common in older dogs, but all can be treated to help the dog live as many happy, comfortable years as possible. Just as in people, medical management is more effective (and less expensive) when you catch things early.

SELECTING A VETERINARIAN
There is probably no more important decision that you will make regarding your pet's healthcare than the selection of his doctor. Your pet's veterinarian will be a pediatrician, family-practice physician and gerontologist, depending on the dog's life stage, and will be the individual who makes recommendations regarding issues such as when specialists need to be consulted, when diagnostic testing and/or therapeutic intervention is needed and when you will need to seek outside emergency and critical-care services. Your vet will act as your advocate and liaison throughout these processes.

Everyone has his own idea about what to look for in a vet, an individual who will play a big role in his dog's (and, of course, his own) life for many years to come. For some, it is the compassionate caregiver with whom they hope to develop a professional relationship to span the lifetime of their dogs and even their future pets. For others, they are seeking a clinician with keen diagnostic and therapeutic insight who can deliver state-of-the-art healthcare. Still others need a veterinary facility that is open evenings and weekends, is in close proximity or provides mobile veterinary services to accommodate their schedules; these people may not much mind that their dogs might see different veterinarians on each visit. Just as we have different reasons for selecting our own healthcare professionals (e.g., covered by insurance plan, expert in field, convenient location, etc.), we should not expect that there is a one-size-fits-all recommendation for selecting a veterinarian and veterinary practice. The best advice is to be honest in your assessment of what you expect from a veterinary practice and to conscientiously research the options in your area. You will quickly appreciate that not all veterinary practices are the same, and you will be happiest with one that truly meets your needs.

There is another point to be considered in the selection of veterinary services. Not that long ago, a single veterinarian would attempt to

Thorough physical exams on a regular basis throughout the dog's life are important to ensure overall health and catch any problems early on.

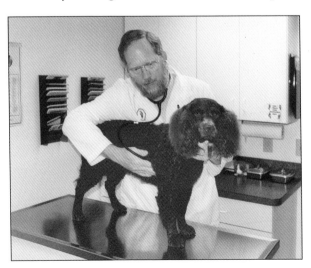

manage all medical and surgical issues as they arose. That was often problematic, because veterinarians are trained in many species and many diseases, and it was just impossible for general veterinary practitioners to be experts in every species, every breed, every field and every ailment. However, just as in the human healthcare fields, specialization has allowed general practitioners to concentrate on primary healthcare delivery, especially wellness and the prevention of infectious diseases, and to utilize a network of specialists to assist in the management of conditions that require specific expertise and experience. Thus there are now many types of veterinary specialists, including dermatologists, cardiologists, ophthalmologists, surgeons, internists, oncologists, neurologists, behaviorists, criticalists and others to help primary-care veterinarians deal with complicated medical challenges. In most cases, specialists see cases referred by primary-care veterinarians, make diagnoses and set up management plans. From there, the animals' ongoing care is returned to their primary-care veterinarians. This important team approach to your pet's medical-care needs has provided opportunities for advanced care and an unparalleled level of quality to be delivered.

With all of the opportunities for your AWS to receive high-quality veterinary medical care, there is another topic that needs to be addressed at the same time—cost. It's been said that you can have excellent healthcare or inexpensive healthcare, but never both; this is as true in veterinary medicine as it is in human medicine. While veterinary costs are a fraction of what the same services cost in the human healthcare arena, it is still difficult to deal with unanticipated medical costs, especially since they can easily creep into hundreds or even thousands of dollars if specialists or emergency services become involved. However, there are ways of managing these risks. The easiest is to buy pet health insurance and realize that its foremost purpose is not to cover routine healthcare visits but rather to serve as an umbrella for those rainy days when your pet needs medical care and you don't want to worry about whether or not you can afford that care.

Pet insurance policies are very cost-effective (and very inexpensive by human health-insurance standards), but make sure that you buy the policy long before you intend to use it (preferably starting in puppyhood, because coverage will exclude pre-existing conditions) and that you are actually buying an indemnity insurance plan from an insurance company that is regulated by your state or province. Many insurance policy look-alikes are actually discount clubs that are redeemable only at specific locations and for specific services. An indemnity plan covers your pet at almost all veterinary, specialty and emergency practices and is an excellent way to manage your pet's ongoing healthcare needs.

VACCINATIONS AND INFECTIOUS DISEASES

There has never been an easier time to prevent a variety of infectious diseases in your dog, but the advances we've made in veterinary medicine come with a price—choice. Now while it may seem that choice is a good thing (and it is), it has never been more difficult for the pet owner (or the veterinarian) to make an informed decision about the best way to protect pets through vaccination.

Years ago, it was just accepted that puppies got a starter series of vaccinations and then annual "boosters" throughout their lives to keep them protected. As more and more vaccines became available, consumers wanted the convenience of having all of that protection in a single injection. The result was "multivalent" vaccines that crammed a lot of protection into a single syringe. The manufacturers' recommendations were to give the vaccines annually, and this was a simple enough protocol to follow. However, as veterinary medicine has become more sophisticated and we have started looking more at healthcare quandaries rather than convenience, it became necessary to reevaluate the situation and deal with some tough questions. It is important to realize that whether or not to use a particular vaccine depends on the risk of contracting the disease against which it protects, the severity of the disease if it is contracted, the duration of immunity provided by the vaccine, the safety of the product and the needs of the individual animal. In a very general sense, rabies, distemper, hepatitis and parvovirus are considered core vaccine needs, while parainfluenza, *Bordetella bronchiseptica*, leptospirosis, coronavirus and borreliosis (Lyme disease) are considered non-core needs and best reserved for animals that demonstrate reasonable risk of contracting the diseases.

NEUTERING/SPAYING

Sterilization procedures (neutering for males/spaying for females) are meant to accomplish several purposes. While the underlying premise is to address the risk of pet overpopulation, there are also some medical and behavioral benefits to the surgeries as well. For females, spaying prior to the first estrus (heat cycle) leads to a marked reduction in the risk of mammary cancer. There also will be no manifestations of "heat" to attract male dogs and no bleeding in the house. For males, there is prevention of testicular cancer and a reduction in the risk of prostate problems. In both sexes there may be some limited

reduction in aggressive behaviors toward other dogs, and some diminishing of urine marking, roaming and mounting.

While neutering and spaying do indeed prevent animals from contributing to pet overpopulation, even no-cost and low-cost neutering options have not eliminated the problem. Perhaps one of the main reasons for this is that individuals who intentionally breed their dogs and those who allow their animals to run at large are the main causes of unwanted offspring. Also, animals in shelters are often there because they were abandoned or relinquished, not because they came from unplanned matings. Neutering/spaying is important, but it should be considered in the context of the real causes of animals' ending up in shelters and eventually being euthanized.

One of the important considerations regarding neutering is that it is a surgical procedure. This sometimes gets lost in discussions of low-cost procedures and commoditization of the process. In females, spaying is specifically referred to as an ovariohysterectomy. In this procedure, a midline incision is made in the abdomen and the entire uterus and both ovaries are surgically removed. While this is a major invasive surgical procedure, it usually has few complications, because it is typically performed on healthy young animals. However, it

Common Infectious Diseases

Let's discuss some of the diseases that create the need for vaccination in the first place. Following are the major canine infectious diseases and a simple explanation of each.

Rabies: A devastating viral disease that can be fatal in dogs and people. In fact, vaccination of dogs and cats is an important public-health measure to create a resistant animal buffer population to protect people from contracting the disease. Vaccination schedules are determined on a government level and are not optional for pet owners; rabies vaccination is required by law in all 50 states.

Parvovirus: A severe, potentially life-threatening disease that is easily transmitted between dogs. There are four strains of the virus, but it is believed that there is significant "cross-protection" between strains that may be included in individual vaccines.

Distemper: A potentially severe and life-threatening disease with a relatively high risk of exposure, especially in certain regions. In very high-risk distemper environments, young pups may be vaccinated with human measles vaccine, a related virus that offers cross-protection when administered at four to ten weeks of age.

Hepatitis: Caused by canine adenovirus type 1 (CAV-1), but since vaccination with the causative virus has a higher rate of adverse effects, cross-protection is derived from the use of adenovirus type 2 (CAV-2), a cause of respiratory disease and one of the potential causes of canine cough. Vaccination with CAV-2 provides long-term immunity against hepatitis, but relatively less protection against respiratory infection.

Canine cough: Also called tracheobronchitis, actually a fairly complicated result of viral and bacterial offenders; therefore, even with vaccination, protection is incomplete. Wherever dogs congregate, canine cough will likely be spread among them. Intranasal vaccination with *Bordetella* and parainfluenza is the best safeguard, but the duration of immunity does not appear to be very long, typically a year at most. These are non-core vaccines, but vaccination is sometimes mandated by boarding kennels, obedience classes, dog shows and other places where dogs congregate to try to minimize spread of infection.

Leptospirosis: A potentially fatal disease that is more common in some geographic regions. It is capable of being spread to humans. The disease varies with the individual "serovar," or strain, of *Leptospira* involved. Since there does not appear to be much cross-protection between serovars, protection is only as good as the likelihood that the serovar in the vaccine is the same as the one in the pet's local environment. Problems with *Leptospira* vaccines are that protection does not last very long, side effects are not uncommon and a large percentage of dogs (perhaps 30%) may not respond to vaccination.

Borrelia burgdorferi: The cause of Lyme disease, the risk of which varies with the geographic area in which the pet lives and travels. Lyme disease is spread by deer ticks in the eastern US and western black-legged ticks in the western part of the country, and the risk of exposure is high in some regions. Lameness, fever and inappetence are most commonly seen in affected dogs. The extent of protection from the vaccine has not been conclusively demonstrated.

Coronavirus: This disease has a high risk of exposure, especially in areas where dogs congregate, but it typically causes only mild to moderate digestive upset (diarrhea, vomiting, etc.). Vaccines are available, but the duration of protection is believed to be relatively short and the effectiveness of the vaccine in preventing infection is considered low.

There are many other vaccinations available, including those for *Giardia* and canine adenovirus-1. While there may be some specific indications for their use, and local risk factors to be considered, they are not widely recommended for most dogs.

is major surgery, as any woman who has had a hysterectomy will attest.

In males, neutering has traditionally referred to castration, which involves the surgical removal of both testicles. While still a significant piece of surgery, there is not the abdominal exposure that is required in the female surgery. In addition, there is now a chemical sterilization option, in which a solution is injected into each testicle, leading to atrophy of the sperm-producing cells. This can typically be done under sedation rather than full anesthesia. This is a relatively new approach, and there are no long-term clinical studies yet available.

Neutering/spaying is typically done around six months of age at most veterinary hospitals, although techniques have been pioneered to perform the procedures in animals as young as eight weeks of age. In general, the surgeries on the very young animals are done for the specific reason of sterilizing them before they go to their new homes. This is done in some shelter hospitals for assurance that the animals will definitely not produce any pups. Otherwise, these organizations need to rely on owners to comply with their wishes to have the animals "altered" at a later date, something that does not always happen.

There are some exciting immunocontraceptive "vaccines" currently under development, and

there may be a time when contraception in pets will not require surgical procedures.

HEREDITARY CONCERNS

The American Water Spaniel is a breed that many consider to be generally healthy. That does not mean that the breed is completely free of health issues, but it does mean that you will not find the breed being devastated by any particular health concern. A variety of abnormal health conditions have surfaced over the years and include allergies, cardiac irregularities, Cushing's disease, diabetes, epilepsy, eye disorders, hip dysplasia and hypothyroidism. Many of these diseases have some form of health screening to identify dogs that are affected. When speaking to a prospective breeder, be certain to ask for proof that the sire and dam of the puppy have received clearances from the Orthopedic Foundation for Animals (OFA) concerning hypothyroidism, abnormal cardiac disorders and hip dysplasia and from the Canine Eye Registration Foundation (CERF) for eye disorders.

Another hereditary concern found in the AWS is a skin disorder often referred to as alopecia but more properly termed follicular dysplasia. Alopecia is a scientific term meaning hair loss and can be attributable to numerous causes. Follicular dysplasia is believed to be a genetic condition, but there have been no definitive studies done in the AWS to determine whether or not this is true. With follicular dysplasia, the hair follicles are abnormal and over time the hair falls out or breaks off. When this occurs, the hair does not regenerate and thus areas of baldness occur, most commonly on the neck, the back of the rear legs, the tail and occasionally along the dog's sides. There is no treatment for this condition, and it can be diagnosed with a skin biopsy. Dogs affected by follicular dysplasia, especially severe cases of it, should not be bred.

While follicular dysplasia is a bit of an aesthetic issue, normally it does not cause discomfort for the dog or any other medical problems. In a dog with extensive alopecia brought on by follicular dysplasia, the condition can adversely affect the field dog whether it is used as a waterfowl retriever or upland-flushing dog. Less coat means greater exposure to the elements, and that can reduce the dog's ability to perform in the field. The American Water Spaniel is not the only breed affected by this disorder, or something similar to it, as it is also found in other curly-coated breeds, including the Irish Water Spaniel, Curly-Coated Retriever and Portuguese Water Dog.

The dedication of AWS enthusiasts to the welfare of the breed has probably never been demonstrated better than by the formation of AWS Partners. The organization formed in 2000 to "secure and provide financial and other support for projects that focus charitable, educational and research efforts on dogs in general and the American Water Spaniel in particular." Linda Ford and Beth Lagimoniere founded AWS Partners after they were unable to find American Water Spaniel resources to assist them in researching canine epilepsy, a medical condition that had struck Beth Lagimoniere's dog Keoni, for whom their first project was named. AWS Partners succeeded in establishing a donor-advised fund with the Canine Health Foundation and worked closely with the University of Missouri in its efforts to research some of the underlying causes of canine epilepsy.

Through its efforts the organization has raised well over $10,000 for research that may directly benefit the American Water Spaniel. AWS Partners has been a success because of the dedication that its founders have toward battling health issues in the breed. It continues to be the only organization conducting regular fundraisers and offering educational support regarding health issues to the AWS community and working with the veterinary medical community in an attempt to eliminate health problems found in the American Water Spaniel.

A scanning electron micrograph of a dog flea, *Ctenocephalides canis*, on dog hair.

S. E. M. BY DR. DENNIS KUNKEL, UNIVERSITY OF HAWAII

EXTERNAL PARASITES

FLEAS

Fleas have been around for millions of years and, while we have better tools now for controlling them than at any time in the past, there still is little chance that they will end up on an endangered species list. Actually, they are very well adapted to living on our pets, and they continue to adapt as we make advances.

The female flea can consume 15 times her weight in blood during active reproduction and can lay as many as 40 eggs a day. These eggs are very resistant to the effects of insecticides. They hatch into larvae, which then mature and spin cocoons. The immature fleas reside in this pupal stage until the time is right for feeding. This pupal stage is also very resistant to the effects of insecticides, and pupae can last in the environment without feeding for many months. Newly emergent fleas are attracted to animals by the warmth of the animals' bodies, movement and exhaled carbon dioxide. However, when they first emerge from their cocoons, they orient towards light; thus when an animal passes between a flea and the light source, casting a shadow, the flea pounces and starts to feed. If the animal turns out to be a dog or cat, the reproductive cycle continues. If the flea lands on another type of animal, including a

FLEA PREVENTION FOR YOUR DOG

- Discuss with your veterinarian the safest product to protect your dog, likely in the form of a monthly tablet or a liquid preparation placed on the back of the dog's neck.
- For dogs suffering from flea-bite dermatitis, a shampoo or topical insecticide treatment is required.
- Your lawn and property should be sprayed with an insecticide designed to kill fleas and ticks that lurk outdoors.
- Using a flea comb, check the dog's coat regularly for any signs of parasites.
- Practice good housekeeping. Vacuum floors, carpets and furniture regularly, especially in the areas that the dog frequents, and wash the dog's bedding weekly.
- Follow up house-cleaning with carpet shampoos and sprays to rid the house of fleas at all stages of development. Insect growth regulators are the safest option.

person, the flea will bite but will then look for a more appropriate host. An emerging adult flea can survive without feeding for up to 12 months but, once it tastes blood, it can survive off its host for only 3 to 4 days.

It was once thought that fleas spend most of their lives in the environment, but we now know that fleas won't willingly jump off a dog unless leaping to another dog or when physically removed by brushing, bathing or other manipulation. Flea eggs, on the other hand, are shiny and smooth, and they roll off the animal and into the environment. The eggs, larvae and pupae then exist in the environment, but once the adult finds a susceptible animal, it's home sweet home until the flea is forced to seek refuge elsewhere.

Since adult fleas live on the animal and immature forms survive in the environment, a successful treatment plan must address all stages of the flea life cycle. There are now several safe and effective flea-control products that can be applied on a monthly basis. These include fipronil, imidacloprid, selamectin and permethrin (found in several formulations). Most of these products have significant flea-killing rates within 24 hours. However, none of them will control the immature forms in the environment. To accomplish this, there are a variety of insect growth regulators that can be sprayed into the

THE FLEA'S LIFE CYCLE

What came first, the flea or the egg? This age-old mystery is more difficult to comprehend than the actual cycle of the flea. Fleas usually live only about four months. A female can lay 2,000 eggs in her lifetime.

Egg

After ten days of rolling around your carpet or under your furniture, the eggs hatch into larvae, which feed on various and sundry debris. In days or

Larva

months, depending on the climate, the larvae spin cocoons and develop into the pupal or nymph stage, which quickly develop into fleas.

Pupa

These immature fleas must locate a host within 10 to 14 days or they will die. Only about 1% of the flea population exist as adult fleas, while the other 99% exist as eggs, larvae or pupae.

Adult

PHOTO BY CAROLINA BIOLOGICAL SUPPLY CO.

environment (e.g., pyriproxyfen, methoprene, fenoxycarb) as well as insect development inhibitors such as lufenuron that can be administered. These compounds have no effect on adult fleas, but they stop immature forms from developing into adults. In years gone by, we relied heavily on toxic insecticides (such as organophosphates, organochlorines and carbamates) to manage the flea problem, but today's options are not only much safer to use on our pets but also safer for the environment.

TICKS

Ticks are members of the spider class (arachnids) and are blood-sucking parasites capable of transmitting a variety of diseases, including Lyme disease, ehrlichiosis, babesiosis and Rocky Mountain spotted fever. It's easy to see ticks on your own skin, but it is more of a challenge when your furry companion is affected. Whenever you happen to be planning a stroll in a tick-infested area (especially forests, grassy or wooded areas or parks) be prepared to do a thorough inspection of your dog afterward to search for ticks. Ticks can be tricky,

> ### TICK CONTROL
> Removal of underbrush and leaf litter and the thinning of trees in areas where tick control is desired are recommended. These actions remove the cover and food sources for small animals that serve as hosts for ticks. With continued mowing of grasses in these areas, the probability of ticks' surviving is further reduced. A variety of insecticide ingredients (e.g., resmethrin, carbaryl, permethrin, chlorpyrifos, dioxathion and allethrin) are registered for tick control around the home.

A scanning electron micrograph of the head of a female deer tick, *Ixodes dammini*, a parasitic tick that carries Lyme disease.

so make sure you spend time looking in the ears, between the toes and everywhere else where a tick might hide. Ticks need to be attached for 24–72 hours before they transmit most of the diseases that they carry, so you do have a window of opportunity for some preventive intervention.

Female ticks live to eat and breed. They can lay between 4,000 and 5,000 eggs and they die soon after. Males, on the other hand, live only to mate with the females and continue the process as long as they are able. Most ticks live on multiple hosts before parasitizing dogs. The immature forms typically reside on grass and shrubs, waiting for susceptible animals to walk by. The larvae and nymph stages typically feed on wildlife.

If only a few ticks are present on a dog, they can be plucked out, but it is important to remove the

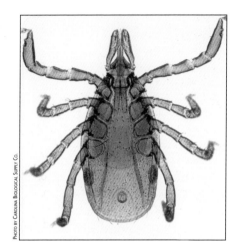

PHOTO BY CAROLINA BIOLOGICAL SUPPLY CO.

entire head and mouthparts, which may be deeply embedded in the skin. This is best accomplished with forceps designed especially for this purpose; fingers can be used but should be protected with rubber gloves, plastic wrap or at least a paper towel. The tick should be grasped as closely as possible to the animal's skin and should be pulled upward with steady, even pressure. Do not squeeze, crush or puncture the body of the tick or you risk exposure to any disease carried by that tick. Once the ticks have been removed, the sites of attachment should be disinfected. Your hands should then be washed with soap and water to further minimize risk of contagion. The tick should be disposed of in a container of alcohol or household bleach.

MITES

Mites are tiny arachnid parasites that parasitize the skin of dogs. Skin

diseases caused by mites are referred to as "mange," and there are many different forms seen in dogs. These forms are very different from one another, each one warranting an individual description.

Sarcoptic mange, or scabies, is one of the itchiest conditions that affects dogs. The microscopic *Sarcoptes* mites burrow into the superficial layers of the skin and can drive dogs crazy with itchiness. They are also communicable to people, although they can't complete their reproductive cycle on people. In addition to being tiny, the mites also are often difficult to find when trying to make a diagnosis. Skin scrapings from multiple areas are examined microscopically but, even then, sometimes the mites cannot be found.

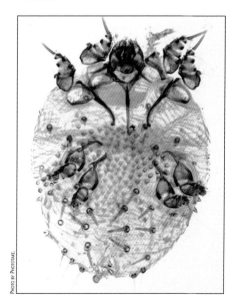

PHOTO BY PHOTOTAKE.

Deer tick, *Ixodes dammini.*

Sarcoptes scabiei, commonly known as the "itch mite."

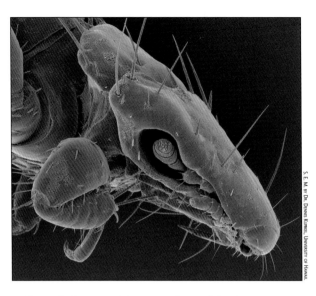

S. E. M. BY DR. DENNIS KUNKEL, UNIVERSITY OF HAWAII

Micrograph of a dog louse, *Heterodoxus spiniger*. Female lice attach their eggs to the hairs of the dog. As the eggs hatch, the larval lice bite and feed on the blood. Lice can also feed on dead skin and hair. This feeding activity can cause hair loss and skin problems.

Illustration of *Demodex folliculoram*.

Fortunately, scabies is relatively easy to treat, and there are a variety of products that will successfully kill the mites. Since the mites can't live in the environment for very long without feeding, a complete cure is usually possible within four to eight weeks.

Cheyletiellosis is caused by a relatively large mite, which sometimes can be seen even without a microscope. Often referred to as "walking dandruff," this also causes itching, but not usually as profound as with scabies. While *Cheyletiella* mites can survive somewhat longer in the environment than scabies mites, they too are relatively easy to treat, being responsive to not only the medications used to treat scabies but also often to flea-control products.

Otodectes cynolis is the canine ear mite and is one of the more common causes of mange, especially in young dogs in shelters or pet stores. That's because the mites are typically present in large numbers and are quickly spread to nearby animals. The mites rarely do much harm but can be difficult to eradicate if the treatment regimen is not comprehensive. While many try to treat the condition with ear drops only, this is the most common cause of treatment failure. Ear drops cause the mites to simply move out of the ears and as far away as possible (usually to the base of the tail) until the insecticide levels in the ears drop to an acceptable level—then it's back to business as usual! The successful treatment of ear mites requires treating all animals in the household with a systemic insecticide, such as selamectin, or a combination of miticidal ear drops combined with whole-body flea-control preparations.

Demodicosis, sometimes referred to as red mange, can be one of the most difficult forms of mange to treat. Part of the problem has to do with the fact that the mites live in the hair follicles and they are relatively well shielded from topical and systemic products. The main issue, however, is that demodectic mange typically results only when there is some underlying

ILLUSTRATION BY PHOTOTAKE

process interfering with the dog's immune system.

Since *Demodex* mites are normal residents of the skin of mammals, including humans, there is usually a mite population explosion only when the immune system fails to keep the number of mites in check. In young animals, the immune deficit may be transient or may reflect an actual inherited immune problem. In older animals, demodicosis is usually seen only when there is another disease hampering the immune system, such as diabetes, cancer, thyroid problems or the use of immune-suppressing drugs. Accordingly, treatment involves not only trying to kill the mange mites but also discerning what is interfering with immune function and correcting it if possible.

Chiggers represent several different species of mite that don't parasitize dogs specifically, but do latch on to passersby and can cause irritation. The problem is most prevalent in wooded areas in the late summer and fall. Treatment is not difficult, as the mites do not complete their life cycle on dogs and are susceptible to a variety of miticidal products.

MOSQUITOES

Mosquitoes have long been known to transmit a variety of diseases to people, as well as just being biting pests during warm weather. They also pose a real risk to pets. Not

only do they carry deadly heartworms but recently there also has been much concern over their involvement with West Nile virus. While we can avoid heartworm with the use of preventive medications, there are no such preventives for West Nile virus. The only method of prevention in endemic areas is active mosquito control. Fortunately, most dogs that have been exposed to the virus only developed flu-like symptoms and, to date, there have not been the large number of reported deaths in canines as seen in some other species.

MOSQUITO REPELLENT
Low concentrations of DEET (less than 10%), found in many human mosquito repellents, have been safely used in dogs but, in these concentrations, probably give only about two hours of protection. DEET may be safe in these small concentrations, but since it is not licensed for use on dogs, there is no research proving its safety for dogs. Products containing permethrin give the longest-lasting protection, perhaps two to four weeks. As DEET is not licensed for use on dogs, and both DEET and permethrin can be quite toxic to cats, appropriate care should be exercised. Other products, such as those containing oil of citronella, also have some mosquito-repellent activity, but typically have a relatively short duration of action.

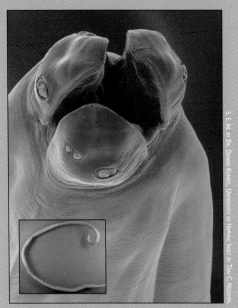

The ascarid roundworm *Toxocara canis*, showing the mouth with three lips. INSET: Photomicrograph of the roundworm *Ascaris lumbricoides*.

The hookworm *Ancylostoma caninum* infests the intestines of dogs. INSET: Note the row of hooks at the posterior end, used to anchor the worm to the intestinal wall.

INTERNAL PARASITES: WORMS

ASCARIDS

Ascarids are intestinal roundworms that rarely cause severe disease in dogs. Nonetheless, they are of major public health significance because they can be transferred to people. Sadly, it is children who are most commonly affected by the parasite, probably from inadvertently ingesting ascarid-contaminated soil. In fact, many yards and children's sandboxes contain appreciable numbers of ascarid eggs. So, while ascarids don't bite dogs or latch onto their intestines to suck blood, they do cause some nasty medical conditions in children and are best eradicated from our furry friends. Because pups can start passing ascarid eggs by three weeks of age, most parasite-control programs begin at two weeks of age and are repeated every two weeks until pups are eight weeks old. It is important to realize that bitches can pass ascarids to their pups even if they test negative prior to whelping. Accordingly, bitches are best treated at the same time as the pups.

HOOKWORMS

Unlike ascarids, hookworms do latch onto a dog's intestinal tract and can cause significant loss of blood and protein. Similar to ascarids, hookworms can be transmitted to humans, where they cause a condition known as cutaneous larval migrans. Dogs can become infected either by consuming the infective larvae or by the larvae's penetrating the skin directly. People most often get infected when they are lying on the ground (such as on a beach) and the larvae penetrate the skin. Yes, the larvae can penetrate through a beach blanket. Hookworms are typically susceptible to the same medications used to treat ascarids.

HEARTWORMS

Heartworm disease is caused by the parasite *Dirofilaria immitis* and is seen in dogs around the world. A member of the roundworm group, it is spread between dogs by the bite of an infected mosquito. The

WORM-CONTROL GUIDELINES

- Practice sanitary habits with your dog and home.
- Clean up after your dog and don't let him sniff or eat other dogs' droppings.
- Control insects and fleas in the dog's environment. Fleas, lice, cockroaches, beetles, mice and rats can act as hosts for various worms.
- Prevent dogs from eating uncooked meat, raw poultry and dead animals.
- Keep dogs and children from playing in sand and soil.
- Kennel dogs on cement or gravel; avoid dirt runs.
- Administer heartworm preventives regularly.
- Have your vet examine your dog's stools at your annual visits.
- Select a boarding kennel carefully so as to avoid contamination from other dogs or an unsanitary environment.
- Prevent dogs from roaming. Obey local leash laws.

Ascarid *Rhabditis*

Hookworm *Ancylostoma caninum*

Tapeworm *Dipylidium caninum*

Heartworm *Dirofilaria immitis*

mosquito injects infective larvae into the dog's skin with its bite, and these larvae develop under the skin for a period of time before making their way to the heart. There they develop into adults, which grow and create blockages of the heart, lungs and major blood vessels there. They also start producing offspring (microfilariae), and these microfilariae circulate in the bloodstream, waiting to hitch a ride when the next mosquito bites. Once in the mosquito, the microfilariae develop into infective larvae and the entire process is repeated.

When dogs get infected with heartworm, over time they tend to develop symptoms associated with heart disease, such as coughing, exercise intolerance and potentially many other manifestations. Diagnosis is confirmed by either seeing the microfilariae themselves in blood samples or using immunologic tests (antigen testing) to identify the presence of adult heartworms. Since antigen tests measure the presence of adult heartworms and microfilarial tests measure offspring produced by adults, neither are positive until six to seven months after the initial infection. However, the beginning of damage can occur by fifth-stage larvae as early as three months after infection. Thus it is possible for dogs to be harboring problem-causing larvae for up to three months before either type of test would identify an infection.

The good news is that there are great protocols available for preventing heartworm in dogs. Testing is critical in the process, and it is important to understand the benefits as well as the limitations of such testing. All dogs six months of age or older that have not been on continuous heartworm-preventive medication should be screened with microfilarial or antigen tests. For dogs receiving preventive medication, periodic antigen testing helps assess the

The dog tapeworm *Taenia pisiformis*.

S. E. M. BY DR. DENNIS KUNKEL, UNIVERSITY OF HAWAII.

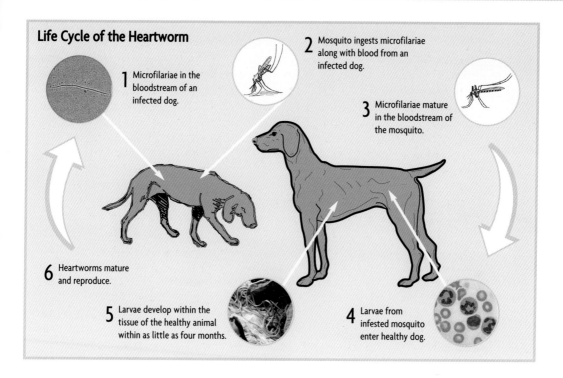

Life Cycle of the Heartworm

1 Microfilariae in the bloodstream of an infected dog.

2 Mosquito ingests microfilariae along with blood from an infected dog.

3 Microfilariae mature in the bloodstream of the mosquito.

4 Larvae from infested mosquito enter healthy dog.

5 Larvae develop within the tissue of the healthy animal within as little as four months.

6 Heartworms mature and reproduce.

effectiveness of the preventives. The American Heartworm Society guidelines suggest that annual retesting may not be necessary when owners have absolutely provided continuous heartworm prevention. Retesting on a two- to three-year interval may be sufficient in these cases. However, your veterinarian will likely have specific guidelines under which heartworm preventives will be prescribed, and many prefer to err on the side of safety and usually retest annually.

It is indeed fortunate that heartworm is relatively easy to prevent, because treatments can be as life-threatening as the disease itself. Treatment requires a two-step process that kills the adult heartworms first and then the microfilariae. Prevention is obviously preferable; this involves a once-monthly oral or topical treatment. The most common oral preventives include ivermectin (not suitable for some breeds), moxidectin and milbemycin oxime; the once-a-month topical drug selamectin provides heartworm protection in addition to flea, some types of tick and other parasite controls.

THE **ABC**s OF
Emergency Care

Abrasions
Clean wound with running water or 3% hydrogen peroxide. Pat dry with gauze and spray with antibiotic. Do not cover.

Animal Bites
Clean area with soap and saline solution or water. Apply pressure to any bleeding area. Apply antibiotic ointment. Identify animal and contact the vet.

Antifreeze Poisoning
Induce vomiting and take dog to the vet.

Bee Sting
Remove stinger and apply soothing lotion or cold compress; give antihistamine in proper dosage.

Bleeding
Apply pressure directly to wound with gauze or towel for five to ten minutes. If wound does not stop bleeding, wrap wound with gauze and adhesive tape.

Bloat/Gastric Torsion
Immediately take the dog to the vet or emergency clinic; phone from car. No time to waste.

Burns
Chemical: Bathe dog with water and pet shampoo. Rinse in saline solution. Apply antibiotic ointment.

Acid: Rinse with water. Apply one part baking soda, two parts water to affected area.

Alkali: Rinse with water. Apply one part vinegar, four parts water to affected area.

Electrical: Apply antibiotic ointment. Seek veterinary assistance immediately.

Choking
If the dog is on the verge of collapsing, wedge a solid object, such as the handle of a screwdriver, between molars on one side of the mouth to keep mouth open. Pull tongue out. Use long-nosed pliers or fingers to remove foreign object. Do not push the object down the dog's throat. For small or medium dogs, hold dog upside down by hind legs and shake firmly to dislodge foreign object.

Chlorine Ingestion
With clean water, rinse the mouth and eyes. Give the dog water to drink; contact the vet.

Constipation
Feed dog 2 tablespoons bran flakes with each meal. Encourage drinking water. Mix $1/4$-teaspoon mineral oil in dog's food.

Diarrhea
Withhold food for 12 to 24 hours. Feed dog anti-diarrheal with eyedropper. When feeding resumes, feed one part boiled hamburger, one part plain cooked rice, $1/4$- to $3/4$-cup four times daily. Contact vet if persists longer than 24 hours.

Dog Bite
Snip away hair around puncture wound; clean with 3% hydrogen peroxide; apply tincture of iodine. Identify biting dog and contact the vet. If wound appears deep, take the dog to the vet.

Frostbite
Wrap the dog in a heavy blanket. Warm affected area with a warm bath for ten minutes. Red color to skin will return with circulation; if tissues are pale after 20 minutes, contact the vet.

Use a portable, durable container large enough to contain all items.

Heat Stroke
Partially submerge the dog in cold water; if no response within ten minutes, contact the vet.

Hot Spots
Mix 2 packets Domeboro® with 2 cups water. Saturate cloth with mixture and apply to hot spots for 15 to 30 minutes. Apply antibiotic ointment. Repeat every six to eight hours.

Poisonous Plants
Wash affected area with soap and water. Cleanse with alcohol. For foxtail/grass, apply antibiotic ointment. Contact the vet if plant is ingested.

Rat Poison Ingestion
Induce vomiting. Keep dog calm, maintain dog's normal body temperature (use blanket or heating pad). Get to the vet for antidote.

Shock
Keep the dog calm and warm; call for veterinary assistance.

Snake Bite
If possible, bandage the area and apply pressure. If the area is not conducive to bandaging, use ice to control bleeding. Get immediate help from the vet.

Tick Removal
Apply flea and tick spray directly on tick. Wait one minute. Using tweezers or wearing plastic gloves, apply constant pull while grasping tick's body. Apply antibiotic ointment.

Vomiting
Restrict dog's water intake; offer a few ice cubes. Withhold food for next meal. Contact vet if vomiting persists longer than 24 hours.

DOG OWNER'S FIRST-AID KIT
- ❏ **Gauze bandages/swabs**
- ❏ **Adhesive and non-adhesive bandages**
- ❏ **Antibiotic powder**
- ❏ **Antiseptic wash**
- ❏ **Hydrogen peroxide 3%**
- ❏ **Antibiotic ointment**
- ❏ **Lubricating jelly**
- ❏ **Rectal thermometer**
- ❏ **Nylon muzzle**
- ❏ **Scissors and forceps**
- ❏ **Eyedropper**
- ❏ **Syringe**
- ❏ **Anti-bacterial/fungal solution**
- ❏ **Saline solution**
- ❏ **Antihistamine**
- ❏ **Cotton balls**
- ❏ **Nail clippers**
- ❏ **Screwdriver/pen knife**
- ❏ **Flashlight**
- ❏ **Emergency phone numbers**

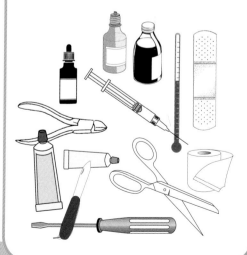

AMERICAN WATER SPANIEL

When we bring home a puppy, full of the energy and exuberance that accompanies youth, we hope for a long, happy and fulfilling relationship with the new family member. Even when we adopt an older dog, we look forward to the years of companionship ahead with a new canine friend. However, aging is inevitable for all creatures, and there will come a time when your American Water Spaniel reaches his senior years and will need special considerations and attention to his care.

WHEN IS MY DOG A "SENIOR"?
In general, pure-bred dogs are considered to have achieved senior status when they reach 75% of their breed's average lifespan, with lifespan being based on breed size along with breed-specific factors. Your American Water Spaniel has an average lifespan of 12 to 14 years and is considered a senior citizen by the time he is 10 years old.

Obviously, the old "seven dog years to one human year" theory is not exact. In puppyhood, a dog's year is actually comparable to more than seven human years, considering the puppy's rapid growth during his first year. Then, in adulthood, the ratio decreases. Regardless, the more viable rule of thumb is that the larger the dog, the shorter his expected lifespan. Of course, this can vary among individual dogs, with many living longer than expected, which we hope is the case!

ADAPTING TO AGE

As dogs age and their once-keen senses begin to deteriorate, they can experience stress and confusion. However, dogs are very adaptable, and most can adjust to deficiencies in their sight and hearing. As these processes often deteriorate gradually, the dog makes adjustments gradually, too. Because dogs become so familiar with the layout of their homes and yards, and with their daily routines, they are able to get around even if they cannot see or hear as well. Help your senior dog by keeping things consistent around the house. Keep up with your regular times for walking and potty trips, and do not relocate his crate or rearrange the furniture. Your dog is a very adaptable creature and can make compensation for his diminished ability, but you want to help him along the way and not make changes that will cause him confusion.

WHAT ARE THE SIGNS OF AGING?

By the time your dog has reached his senior years, you will know him very well, so the physical and behavioral changes that accompany aging should be noticeable to you. Humans and dogs share the most obvious physical sign of aging: gray hair. Graying often occurs first on the muzzle and face, around the eyes. Other telltale signs are the dog's overall decrease in activity. Your older dog might be more content to nap and rest, and he may not show the same old enthusiasm when it's time to play in the yard or go for a walk. Other physical signs include significant weight loss or gain; more labored movement; skin and coat problems, possibly hair loss; sight and/or hearing problems; changes in toileting habits, perhaps seeming "unhousebroken" at times; and tooth decay, bad breath or other mouth problems.

There are behavioral changes that go along with aging, too. There are numerous causes for behavioral changes. Sometimes a dog's apparent confusion results from a physical change like diminished sight or hearing. If his confusion causes him to be afraid, he may act aggressively or defensively. He may sleep more frequently because his daily walks, though shorter now, tire him out. He may begin to experi-

Even though this American Water Spaniel's muzzle is starting to show some gray, he still looks alert and ready to work. "Old age" is a relative term for dogs as well as for humans.

ence separation anxiety or, conversely, become less interested in petting and attention.

There also are clinical conditions that cause behavioral changes in older dogs. One such condition is known as canine cognitive dysfunction (familiarly known as "old-dog" syndrome). It can be frustrating for an owner whose dog is affected with cognitive dysfunction, as it can result in behavioral changes of all types, most seemingly unexplainable. Common changes include the dog's forgetting aspects of the daily routine, such as times to eat, go out for walks, relieve himself and the like. Along the same lines, you may take your dog out at the regular time for a potty trip and he may have no idea why he is there. Sometimes a placid dog will begin to show aggressive or possessive tendencies or, conversely, a hyperactive dog will start to "mellow out."

Disease also can be the cause of behavioral changes in senior dogs. Hormonal problems (Cushing's disease is common in older dogs), diabetes and thyroid disease can cause increased appetite, which can lead to aggression related to food guarding. It's better to be proactive with your senior dog, making more frequent trips to the vet if necessary and having bloodwork done to test for the diseases that can commonly befall older dogs.

This is not to say that, as dogs age, they all fall apart physically and become nasty in personality. The aforementioned changes are discussed to alert owners to the things that may happen as their dogs get older. Many hardy dogs remain active and alert well into old age. However, it can be frustrating and heartbreaking for owners to see their beloved dogs change physically and temperamentally. Just know that it's the same American Water Spaniel under there, and that he still loves you and appreciates your care, which he needs now more than ever.

CARING FOR MY AGING DOG

Again, every dog is an individual in terms of aging. Your dog might reach the estimated "senior" age for the AWS and show no signs of slowing down. However, even if he shows no outward signs of aging, he should begin a senior-care program once he reaches the determined age. He may not show it, but he's not a pup anymore! By providing him with extra attention to his veterinary care at this age, you will be practicing good preventive medicine, ensuring that the rest of your dog's life will be as long, active, happy and healthy as possible. If you do notice indications of aging, such as graying and/or changes in sleeping, eating or toileting habits, this is a sign to set up a senior-care visit with your vet right away to make sure that these changes are not related to any health problems.

To start, senior dogs should visit the vet twice yearly for exams, routine tests and overall evaluations. Many veterinarians have special screening programs especially for senior dogs that can include a thorough physical exam; blood test to determine complete blood count; serum biochemistry test, which screens for liver, kidney and blood problems as well as cancer; urinalysis; and dental exams. With these tests, it can be determined whether your dog has any health problems; the results also establish a baseline for your pet against which future test results can be compared.

In addition to these tests, your vet may suggest additional testing, including an EKG, tests for glaucoma and other problems of the eye, chest x-rays, screening for tumors, blood pressure test, test for thyroid function and screening for parasites and reassessment of his preventive program. Your vet also will ask you questions about your dog's diet and activity level, what you feed and the amounts that you feed. This information, along with his evaluation of the dog's overall condition, will enable him to suggest proper dietary changes, if needed.

RUBDOWN REMEDY

A good remedy for an aching dog is to give him a gentle massage each day or even a few times a day if possible. This can be especially beneficial before your dog gets out of his bed in the morning. Just as in humans, massage can decrease pain in dogs, whether the dog is arthritic or just afflicted by the stiffness that accompanies old age. Gently massage his joints and limbs, as well as petting him on his entire body. This can help his circulation and flexibility and ease any joint or muscle aches. Massaging your dog has benefits for you, too; in fact, just petting our dogs can cause reduced levels of stress and lower our blood pressure. Massage and petting also help you find any previously undetected lumps, bumps or abnormalities. Often these are not visible and only turn up by being felt.

This may seem like quite a work-up for your pet, but veterinarians advise that older dogs need more frequent attention so that any health problems can be detected as early as possible. Serious conditions like kidney disease, heart disease and cancer may not present outward symptoms, or the problem may go undetected if the symptoms are mistaken by owners as just part of the aging process.

There are some conditions more common in elderly dogs that are difficult to ignore. Cognitive dysfunction shares much in common with senility and Alzheimer's disease, and dogs are not immune. Dogs can become confused and/or disoriented, lose their house-training, have abnormal sleep-wake cycles and interact differently with their owners. Be heartened by the fact that, in some ways, there are more treatment options for dogs with cognitive dysfunction than for people with similar conditions. There is good evidence that continued stimulation in the form of games, play, training and exercise can help to maintain cognitive function. There are also medications (such as seligiline) and antioxidant-fortified senior diets that have been shown to be beneficial.

Cancer is also a condition more common in the elderly. Almost all of the cancers seen in people are also seen in pets. While we can't control the effects of secondhand smoke, lung cancer, which is a major killer in humans, is relatively rare in dogs. If pets are getting regular physical examinations, cancers are often detected early. There are a variety of cancer therapies available today, and many pets continue to live happy lives with appropriate treatment.

Degenerative joint disease, often referred to as arthritis, is another malady common to both elderly dogs and humans. A lifetime of wear and tear on joints and running around at play eventually take toll and result in stiffness and difficulty in getting around. As dogs live longer and healthier lives, it is natural that they should eventually feel some of the effects of aging. Once again, if regular veterinary care has been available, your pet was not carrying extra pounds all those years and wearing those joints out before their time. If your pet was unfortunate enough to inherit hip dysplasia, osteochondritis dissecans or any of the other developmental orthopedic diseases, battling the onset of degenerative joint disease was probably a longstanding goal. In any case, there are now many effective remedies for managing degenerative joint disease and a number of remarkable surgeries as well.

Aside from the extra veterinary care, there is much you can do at home to keep your older dog in good condition. The dog's diet is an important factor. If your dog's appetite decreases, he will not be getting the nutrients he needs. He also will lose weight, which is unhealthy for a dog at a proper weight. Conversely, an older dog's metabolism is slower and he usually exercises less, but he should not be allowed to become obese. Obesity in an older dog is especially risky, because extra pounds mean extra stress on the body, increasing his vulnerability to heart disease. Additionally, the extra pounds make it harder for the dog to move about.

You should discuss age-related feeding changes with your vet. For a dog who has lost interest in food, it may be suggested to try some different types of food until you find something new that the dog likes. For an obese dog, a "light"-formula dog food or reducing food portions may be advised, along with exercise appropriate to his physical condition and energy level.

As for exercise, the senior dog should not be allowed to become a "couch potato" despite his old age. He may not be able to handle the morning run, long walks and vigorous games of fetch, but he still needs to get up and get moving. Keep up with your daily walks, but keep the distances shorter and let your dog set the pace. If he gets to the point where he's not up for walks, let him stroll around the yard. On the other hand, many dogs remain very active in their senior years, so base changes to the exercise program on your own individual dog and what he's capable of. Don't worry, your American Water Spaniel will let you know when it's time to rest.

Keep up with your grooming routine as you always have. Be extra diligent about checking the skin and coat for problems. Older dogs can experience thinning coats as a normal aging process, but they can also lose hair as a result of medical problems. Some thinning is normal, but patches of age-related baldness or the loss of significant amounts of hair is not.

Hopefully, you've been regular with brushing your dog's teeth throughout his life. Healthy teeth directly affect overall good health. We already know that bacteria from gum infections can enter the dog's body through the damaged gums and travel to the organs. At a stage in life when his organs don't function as well as they used to, you don't want anything to put additional strain on them. Clean teeth also contribute to a healthy immune system. Offering the dental-type chews in addition to tooth-brushing can help, as they

remove plaque and tartar as the dog chews.

Along with the same good care you've given him all of his life, pay a little extra attention to your dog in his senior years and keep up with twice-yearly trips to the vet. The sooner a problem is uncovered, the greater the chances of a full recovery.

SAYING GOODBYE

While you can help your dog live as long a life as possible, you can't help him live forever. A dog's lifespan is short when compared to that of a human, so it is inevitable that pet owners will experience loss. To many, losing a beloved dog is like losing a family member. Our dogs are part of our lives every day; they are our true loyal friends and always seem to know when it's time to comfort us, to celebrate with us or to just provide the company of a caring friend. Even when we know that our dog is nearing his final days, we can never quite prepare for his being gone.

Many dogs live out long lives and simply die of old age. Others unfortunately are taken suddenly by illness or accident, and still others find their senior years compromised by disease and physical problems. In some of these cases, owners find themselves having to make difficult decisions.

SHOWING YOUR

AMERICAN WATER SPANIEL

Is dog showing in your blood? Are you excited by the idea of gaiting your handsome AWS around the ring to the thunderous applause of an enthusiastic audience? Are you certain that your beloved AWS is flawless? You are not alone! Every loving owner thinks that his dog has no faults, or too few to mention. No matter how many times an owner reads the breed standard, he cannot find any faults in his aristocratic companion dog. If this sounds like you, and if you are considering entering your AWS in a dog show, here are some basic questions to ask yourself:

- Did you purchase a "show-quality" puppy from the breeder?
- Is your puppy old enough to show?
- Does the puppy exhibit correct show type for his breed?
- Does your puppy have any disqualifying faults?
- Is your AWS registered with the American Kennel Club or the UKC?
- How much time do you have to devote to training, grooming, conditioning and exhibiting your dog?

- Do you understand the rules and regulations of a dog show?
- Do you have time to learn how to show your dog properly?
- Do you have the financial resources to invest in showing your dog?
- Will you show the dog yourself or hire a professional handler, if permissible?
- Do you have a vehicle that can accommodate your weekend trips to the dog shows?

Success in the show ring requires more than a handsome face, a waggy tail and a pocketful of liver. Even though dog shows can be exciting and enjoyable, the sport of conformation makes great demands on the exhibitors and the dogs. Winning exhibitors live for their dogs, devoting time and money to their dogs' presentation, conditioning and training. Very few novices, even those with good dogs, will find themselves in the winners' circle, though it does happen. Don't be disheartened, though. Every exhibitor began as a novice and worked his way up to the Group ring. It's the "working your way up" part that you must keep in mind.

Assuming that you have purchased a puppy of the correct type and quality for showing, let's begin to examine the world of showing and what's required to get started. Although the entry fee into a dog show is nominal, there are lots of other hidden costs involved with "finishing" your AWS, that is, making him a champion. Things like equipment, travel, training and conditioning all cost money. A more serious campaign will include fees for a professional handler, boarding, cross-country travel and advertising. Top-winning show dogs can represent a very considerable investment—over $100,000 has been spent in campaigning some dogs. (The investment can be less, of course, for owners who don't use professional handlers.)

Many owners, on the other hand, enter their "average" American Water Spaniels in dog shows for the fun and enjoyment of it. Dog showing makes an absorbing hobby, with many rewards for dogs and owners alike. If you're having fun, meeting other people who share your interests and enjoying the overall experience, you likely will catch the "bug." Once the dog-show bug bites, its effects can last a lifetime; it's certainly much better than a deer tick! Soon you will be envisioning yourself in the center ring at the Westminster Kennel Club Dog Show in New

York City, competing for the prestigious Best in Show cup. This magical dog show is televised annually from Madison Square Garden, and the victorious dog becomes a celebrity overnight.

AKC CONFORMATION SHOWING

GETTING STARTED
Visiting a dog show as a spectator is a great place to start. Pick up the show catalog to find out what time your breed is being shown, who is judging the breed and in which ring the classes will be held. To start, American Water Spaniels

FOR MORE INFORMATION...

For reliable up-to-date information about registration, dog shows and other canine competitions, contact one of the national registries by mail or via the Internet.

American Kennel Club
5580 Centerview Dr., Raleigh, NC 27606-3390
www.akc.org

United Kennel Club
100 E. Kilgore Road, Kalamazoo, MI 49002
www.ukcdogs.com

Canadian Kennel Club
89 Skyway Ave., Suite 100, Etobicoke, Ontario M9W 6R4, Canada
www.ckc.ca

The Kennel Club
1-5 Clarges St., Piccadilly, London W1Y 8AB, UK
www.the-kennel-club.org.uk

go head to head in the ring for the Best in Show award. The American Water Spaniel competes in the Sporting Group.

What most spectators don't understand is the basic idea of conformation. A dog show is often referred as a "conformation" show. This means that the judge should decide how each dog stacks up (conforms) to the breed standard for his given breed: how well does this AWS conform to the ideal representative detailed in the standard? Ideally, this is what happens. In reality, however, this ideal often gets slighted as the judge compares AWS #1 to AWS #2. Again, the ideal is that each dog is judged based on his merits in comparison to his breed standard, not in comparison to the other dogs in the ring. It is easier for judges to compare dogs of the same breed to decide which they think is the better specimen; in the Group and Best in Show ring, however, it is very difficult to compare one breed to another, like apples to oranges. Thus the dog's conformation to the breed standard—not to mention advertising dollars and good handling—is essential to success in conformation shows. The dog described in the standard (the standard for each AKC breed is written and approved by the breed's national parent club and then submitted

compete against other American Water Spaniels, and the winner is selected as Best of Breed by the judge. This is the procedure for each breed. At a group show, all of the Best of Breed winners go on to compete for Group One (first place) in their respective groups. For example, all Best of Breed winners in a given group compete against each other; this is done for all seven groups. Finally, all seven group winners to the AKC for approval) is the perfect dog of that breed, and breeders keep their eye on the standard when they choose which dogs to breed, hoping to get closer and closer to the ideal with each litter.

Another good first step for the novice is to join a dog club. You will be astonished by the many and different kinds of dog clubs in the country, with about 5,000 clubs holding events every year. Most clubs require that prospective new members present two letters of recommendation from existing members. Perhaps you've made some friends visiting a show held by a particular club and you would like to join that club. Dog clubs may specialize in a single breed, like a local or regional AWS club, or in a specific pursuit, such as obedience, tracking or hunting tests. There are all-breed clubs for all dog enthusiasts; they sponsor special training days, seminars on

Each AWS is gaited so that the judge can evaluate movement. This is Ch. Wish N' Well Tarheel Marksman CD, CGC at Westminster.

topics like grooming or handling or lectures on breeding or canine genetics. There are also clubs that specialize in certain types of dogs, like herding dogs, hunting dogs, companion dogs, etc.

A parent club is the national organization, sanctioned by the AKC, which promotes and safeguards its breed in the country. The American Water Spaniel Club, Inc. can be contacted on the Internet at www.americanwaterspaniel-club.org. The parent club holds an annual national specialty show, usually in a different city each year, in which many of the country's top dogs, handlers and breeders gather to compete. At a specialty show, only members of a single breed are invited to participate. There are also

Group specialties, in which all members of a Group are invited. For more information about dog clubs in your area, contact the AKC at www.akc.org on the Internet or write them at their Raleigh, NC addresss.

HOW SHOWS ARE ORGANIZED
Three kinds of conformation shows are offered by the AKC. There is the all-breed show, in which all AKC-recognized breeds can compete; the specialty show, which is for one breed only and usually sponsored by the breed's parent club and the group show, for all breeds in one of the AKC's seven groups. The AWS competes in the Sporting Group.

For a dog to become an AKC champion of record, the dog must earn 15 points at shows. The points must be awarded by at least three different judges and must include two "majors" under different judges. A "major" is a three-, four- or five-point win, and the number of points per win is determined by the number of dogs competing in the show on that day. (Dogs that are absent or are excused are not counted.) The number of points that are awarded varies from breed to breed. More dogs are needed to attain a major in more popular breeds, and fewer dogs are needed in less popular breeds. Yearly, the AKC evaluates the

The judge will evaluate each dog individually, including a hands-on inspection of the dog's mouth, head and body.

number of dogs in competition in each division (there are 14 divisions in all, based on geography) and may or may not change the numbers of dogs required for each number of points. The AWS attracts numerically proportionate representation at all-breed shows.

Only one dog and one bitch of each breed can win points at a given show. There are no "co-ed" classes except for champions of record. Dogs and bitches do not compete against each other until they are champions. Dogs that are not champions (referred to as "class dogs") compete in one of five classes. The class in which a dog is entered depends on age and previous show wins. First there is the Puppy Class (sometimes divided further into classes for 6- to 9-month-olds and 9- to 12-month-olds); next is the Novice Class (for dogs that have no points toward their championship and whose only first-place wins have come in the Puppy Class or the Novice Class, the latter class limited to three first places); then there is the American-bred Class (for dogs bred in the US); the Bred-by-Exhibitor Class (for dogs handled by their breeders or by immediate family members of their breeders) and the Open Class (for any non-champions). Any dog may enter the Open Class, regardless of age or win

history, but to be competitive the dog should be older and have ring experience.

The judge at the show begins judging the male dogs in the Puppy Class(es) and proceeds through the other classes. The judge awards first through fourth place in each class. The first-place winners of each class then compete with one another in the Winners Class to determine Winners Dog. The judge then starts over with the bitches, beginning with the Puppy Class(es) and proceeding up to the Winners Class to award Winners Bitch, just as he did with the dogs. A Reserve Winners Dog and Reserve Winners Bitch are also selected; they could be awarded the points in the case of a disqualification.

Rally obedience is a fun activity you can share with your AWS.

This is Mick "on the scent" during a tracking competition. There is little this breed can't do.

The Winners Dog and Winners Bitch are the two that are awarded the points for their breed. They then go on to compete with any champions of record (often called "specials") of their breed that are entered in the show. The champions may be dogs or bitches; in this class, all are shown together. The judge reviews the Winners Dog and Winners Bitch along with all of the champions to select the Best of Breed winner. The Best of Winners is selected between the Winners Dog and Winners Bitch; if one of these two is selected Best of Breed as well, he or she is automatically determined Best of Winners. Lastly, the judge selects Best of Opposite Sex to the Best of Breed winner. The Best of Breed winner then goes on to the Group competition.

At a group or all-breed show, the Best of Breed winners from each breed are divided into their respective groups to compete against one another for Group One through Group Four. Group One (first place) is awarded to the dog that best lives up to the ideal for his breed as described in the standard. A group judge, therefore, must have a thorough working knowledge of many breed standards. After placements have been made in each Group, the seven Group One winners (from the Sporting Group, Toy Group, Hound Group, etc.) compete against each other for the top honor, Best in Show.

There are different ways to find out about dog shows in your area. The American Kennel Club's monthly magazine, the *American Kennel Gazette,* is accompanied by the *Events Calendar*; this magazine is available through subscription. You can also look on the AKC's and your parent club's websites for information and check the event listings in your local newspaper.

Your AWS must be six months of age or older and registered with the AKC in order to be entered in AKC-sanctioned shows in which there are classes for the AWS. Your AWS also must not possess any disqualifying faults and must be sexually intact. The reason for the latter is simple: dog shows are the proving grounds to determine which dogs and bitches are worthy of being bred. If they cannot be bred, that defeats the purpose! On that note, only dogs that have

CANINE GOOD CITIZEN® PROGRAM

Have you ever considered getting your dog "certified"? The AKC's Canine Good Citizen® Program affords your dog just that opportunity. Your dog shows that he is a well-behaved canine citizen, using the basic training and good manners you have taught him, by taking a series of ten tests that illustrate that he can behave properly at home, in a public place and around other dogs. The tests are administered by participating dog clubs, colleges, 4-H clubs, Scouts and other community groups and are open to all pure-bred and mixed-breed dogs. Upon passing the ten tests, the suffix CGC is then applied to your dog's name.

The ten tests are: 1. Accepting a friendly stranger; 2. Sitting politely for petting; 3. Appearance and grooming; 4. Walking on a lead; 5. Walking through a group of people; 6. Sit, down and stay on command; 7. Coming when called; 8. Meeting another dog; 9. Calm reaction to distractions; 10. Separation from owner.

achieved championships, thus proving their excellent quality, should be bred. If you have spayed or neutered your dog, however, there are many AKC events other than conformation, such as obedience trials, agility trials and the Canine Good Citizen® Program, in which you and your American Water Spaniel can participate.

OTHER TYPES OF COMPETITION

In addition to conformation shows, the AKC holds a variety of other competitive events. Obedience trials, agility trials and tracking trials are open to all breeds, while hunting tests, field trials, lure coursing, herding tests and trials, earthdog tests and coonhound events are limited to specific breeds or groups of breeds. The Junior Showmanship program is offered to aspiring young handlers and their dogs, and the Canine Good Citizen® Program is an all-around good-behavior test open to all dogs, pure-bred and mixed.

OBEDIENCE TRIALS

Mrs. Helen Whitehouse Walker, a Standard Poodle fancier, can be credited with introducing obedience trials to the United States. In the 1930s she designed a series of exercises based on those of the Associated Sheep, Police, Army Dog Society of Great Britain. These exercises were intended to evaluate the working relationship between dog and owner. Since those early days of the sport in the US, obedience trials have grown more and more popular, and now more than 2,000 trials each year attract over 100,000 dogs and their owners. Any dog registered with the AKC, regardless of neutering or other disqualifications that would preclude entry in conformation competition, can participate in obedience trials.

There are three levels of difficulty in obedience competition. The first (and easiest) level is the Novice, in which dogs can earn the Companion Dog (CD) title. The intermediate level is the Open level, in which the Companion Dog Excellent (CDX) title is awarded. The advanced level is the Utility level, in which dogs compete for the Utility Dog (UD) title. Classes at each level are further divided into "A" and "B," with "A" for beginners and "B" for those with more experience. In order to win a title at a given level, a dog must earn three "legs." A "leg" is accomplished when a dog scores 170 or higher (200 is a perfect score). The scoring system gets a little trickier when you understand that a dog must score more than 50% of the points available for each exercise in order to actually earn the points. Available points for each exercise range between 20 and 40.

A dog must complete different exercises at each level of obedience. The Novice exercises are the easiest, with the Open and finally the Utility levels progressing in difficulty.

Examples of Novice exercises are on- and off-lead heeling, a figure-8 pattern, performing a recall (or come), long sit and long down and standing for examination. In the Open level, the Novice-level exercises are required again, but this time without a leash and for longer durations. In addition, the dog must clear a broad jump, retrieve over a jump and drop on recall. In the Utility level, the exercises are quite difficult, including executing basic commands based on hand signals, following a complex heeling pattern, locating articles based on scent discrimination and completing jumps at the handler's direction.

Once he's earned the UD title, a dog can go on to win the prestigious title of Utility Dog Excellent (UDX) by winning "legs" in ten shows. Additionally, Utility Dogs who win "legs" in Open B and Utility B earn points toward the lofty title of Obedience Trial Champion (OTCh.). Established in 1977 by the AKC, this title

Although one of the smallest sporting dogs, the AWS cannot be deterred from succeeding in many areas of competition.

Lynn Morrison and her dog Gunner with a late-season rooster shot in southern Michigan.

requires a dog to earn 100 points as well as 3 first places in a combination of Open B and Utility B classes under 3 different judges. The "brass ring" of obedience competition is the AKC's National Obedience Invitational. This is an exclusive competition for only the cream of the obedience crop. In order to qualify for the invita-tional, a dog must be ranked in either the top 25 all-breeds in obedience or in the top 3 for his breed in obedience. The title at stake here is that of National Obedience Champion (NOC).

AGILITY TRIALS

Agility trials became sanctioned by the AKC in August 1994, when the first licensed agility trials were held. Since that time, agility certainly has grown in popularity by leaps and bounds, literally! The AKC allows all registered breeds (including Miscellaneous Class breeds) to participate, providing the dog is 12 months of age or older. Agility is designed so that the handler demonstrates how well the dog can work at his side. The handler directs his dog through, over, under and around an obstacle course that includes jumps, tires, the dog walk, weave poles, pipe tunnels, collapsed tunnels and more. While working his way through the course, the dog must keep one eye and ear on the handler and the rest of his body on the course. The handler runs along with the dog, giving verbal and hand signals to guide the dog through the course.

The first organization to promote agility trials in the US was the United States Dog Agility Association, Inc. (USDAA). Established in 1986, the USDAA sparked the formation of many member clubs around the country. To participate in USDAA trials, dogs must be at least 18 months of age.

The USDAA and AKC both offer titles to winning dogs, although the exercises and requirements of the two organizations differ. Agility Dog (AD), Advanced Agility Dog (AAD) and Master Agility Dog (MAD) are the titles offered by the USDAA, while the AKC offers Novice Agility (NA), Open Agility (OA), Agility Excellent (AX) and Master Agility Excellent (MX). Beyond these four AKC titles, dogs can win additional titles in "jumper" classes: Jumper with Weave Novice (NAJ), Open (OAJ) and Excellent (MXJ). The ultimate title in AKC agility is MACH, Master Agility Champion. Dogs can continue to add number designations to the MACH title, indicating how many times the dog has met the title's requirements (MACH1, MACH2 and so on).

Agility trials are a great way to keep your dog active, and they will keep you running, too! You should join a local agility club to learn more about the sport. These clubs offer sessions in which you can introduce your dog to the various obstacles as well as training classes to prepare him for competition. In no time, your dog will be climbing A-frames, crossing the dog walk and flying over hurdles, all with you right beside him. Your heart will leap every time your dog jumps through the hoop—and you'll be having just as much (if not more) fun!

HUNTING TESTS

Hunting tests are not competitive like field trials, and participating dogs are judged against a standard, as in a conformation show. The first hunting tests were devised by the North American Hunting Retriever Association (NAHRA) as an alternative to field trials for retriever owners to appreciate their dogs' natural innate ability in the field without the expense and pressure of a formal field trial. The intent of hunting tests is the same as that of field trials: to test the dog's ability in a simulated hunting scenario.

The AKC instituted its hunting tests in June 1985; since then, their popularity has grown tremendously. The AKC offers three titles at hunting tests, Junior Hunter (JH), Senior Hunter (SH) and Master Hunter (MH). Each title requires that the dog earn qualifying "legs" at the tests: the JH requiring four; the SH, five; and the MH, six. In addition to the AKC, the United Kennel Club also offers hunting tests through its affiliate club, the Hunting

Retriever Club, Inc. (HRC), which began the tests in 1984.

In addition to the hunt tests offered by the AKC, HRC and NAHRA, there is another series of working titles offered by the American Water Spaniel Club, Inc. These titles are earned through the AWSC's hunt-test program. Although the rules and regulations resemble many of those found in the various registries, the AWSC hunt tests are truly of the club's own design. This testing program blends elements of spaniel hunt tests with those of the retriever hunt tests. Titles earned do not appear on any registry's official pedigree, but they are well respected just the same. These tests are seldom found outside of the upper Midwest, and owners will have to contact the American Water Spaniel Club, Inc. for details of the program.

AKC Spaniel Hunt Test titles became available to the American Water Spaniel in June, 2005. To earn a title an American Water Spaniel must complete the requirements of the American Kennel Club and must also complete additional requirements

Hunting is in the American Water Spaniel's blood. This AWS proudly sits with his handler and the day's bag.

of the American Water Spaniel
Club, Inc. AKC requirements for
earning a Spaniel Hunt Test title
vary somewhat by the title's level
but generally include finding,
flushing and retrieving birds shot
in the field, successfully
completing a "hunt dead" exercise
where the dog locates a bird that
it did not see flushed or shot from
an area remote to the handler and
at least one water retrieve
including, at the uppermost level,
a blind water retrieve.

The additional requirement
for earning an AKC Spaniel Hunt
Test title imposed by the
American Water Spaniel Club,
Inc. and endorsed by the AKC is
that a dog must successfully pass
two Retrieving Certificate Tests
specific to the title the handler is
seeking. These tests examine the
dog's ability to successfully
retrieve birds from water in the
manner of a non-slip retriever.
Depending upon the title sought,
dogs could be required to make
multiple water retrieves
including a blind retrieve at
distances greater than those
found in the AKC Spaniel Hunt
Test program. Dogs running in
these tests will have a higher
level of precision training and
will have to contend with more
obstacles, distractions and
testing elements than they will
encounter in any AKC Spaniel
Hunt Test. Owners wishing to
find out more about these tests

should contact the American
Water Spaniel Club, Inc.

The testing programs of the
HRC and the NAHRA are
designed to simulate the work
done by a non-slip retriever
during a waterfowl hunt. The
work required varies by the
testing level and ranges from
very basic water and land
retrieves to extensive multiple
marked and blind retrieves on
both land and water. The
distances encountered in these
tests push the extreme limits of a
dog's range and titles of this type
are highly prized, especially for
a medium-sized spaniel. While
there have only been a handful
of American Water Spaniels that
have earned the highest title
available from these testing
groups, it goes to show that with
dedication and perseverance the
American Water Spaniel can run
with the big boys.

An American Water Spaniel
owner wishing to pursue a set of
field titles for his dog should first
determine the type of title—AKC
Spaniel, AWSC or one of the
retriever titles—before becoming
embroiled in a substantial
training program. Because the
working requirements of one
program can impinge upon those
of the other, it is often best to
work primarily on one over the
other. It is this author's belief that
an individual seeking both a
spaniel title and a retriever title is

What more could hunters want in an able, intelligent and dependable all-purpose hunting companion and helper?

better off to pursue the upper-level spaniel and mid-level retriever titles before moving on to the higher level retriever titles.

Working with professional trainers or at least top amateur trainers offering assistance through local training clubs will be the key to success for the average dog owner. In addition, attending training seminars, watching field training videos and reading any of the myriad of books written regarding the field training of spaniels or retrievers will work to improve the American Water Spaniel owner's understanding of the training process.

Acetaminophen 55
Activities 108
—senior dog 138
Adenovirus 119
Adult
—adoption 89
—health 113
—training 88-89
Aggression 60, 90, 118
Agility 19, 30, 108, 150, 153
—trials 146, 148
Aging 115, 134-135
Air travel 85
AKC Gazette 44, 146
All-breed show 146
Allergies 120
Almonds 68
Alopecia 120-121
American Brown 11-12
American Brown Water Spaniel 11
American Kennel Club 13-14, 17, 19, 21, 36, 44, 46, 140, 143, 146, 152
—address 140
—breed standard 40-43
—competitive events 146
—conformation showing 142
—field classification 21
—Spaniel Hunt Test program 21, 153
American Spaniel 11
American Water Spaniel Breeders Association 17
American Water Spaniel Club 13-14
American Water Spaniel Club, Inc. 17, 21, 35, 153
—Retrieving Certificate Tests 21, 34
American Water Spaniel Field Association 18-19
Americana kennels 17
American-bred Class 145
Ancylostoma caninum **128**, **129**
Anemia 68
Annual vet exams 113
Antifreeze 58
Arthritis 138
Ascarid **128**, 129
Ascaris lumbricaides **128**
Attention 97, 99, 104
AWS Partners 121
Barking 28-30
Barth, John and Marilyn 15, 17
Bathing 76-77
Bedding 52, 60, 94
Best in Show 142, 146
Best of Breed 142, 145-146
Best of Opposite Sex 146
Best of Winners 145

Boarding 87
Body language 90, 95, 101
Bones 54
Bordetella 119
Bordetella bronchiseptica 118
Borrelia burgdorferi 119
Borreliosis 118
Bovee, Paul 15, 17
Bowers, Gina 25
Bowls 51
Brayton, Dixie Lee 22
Bred-by-Exhibitor Class 145
Breed standard 37, 40, 142
Breeder 44, 47, 142
—selection 44, 50, 111
Brockman, Father Vaughn 17
Brogden, Thomas 13
California Chocolate Chip **30**
Canadian Kennel Club 140
Cancer 118, 137
Canine cough 119
Canine Eye Registration Foundation 120
Canine Good Citizen® Program 146-147
Canine Health Foundation 121
Canis domesticus 10
Canis lupus **10**
Car travel 85
Cardiac irregularities 46, 120
Champion 144
Chesapeake Bay Retriever 10-11
Chew toys 53-54, 66, 92, 94
Chewing 53, 65
Cheyletiella mites **125**
Cheyletiellosis 125
Chiggers 127
Children 27, 49, 59, 62, 65, 90
Choco Lot Morrison **16**
Class dogs 145
Classes at shows 145
Clubs 142
Coat 30-31, 38
—senior dog 139
Cognitive dysfunction 115, 137
Collars 55, 97
Come 103
Commands 100
—practicing 100, 102
Commitment of ownership 49-50
Companion Dog 147
Competitive events 146
Complete Guide To Bird Dog Training 35
Conformation showing 141-142
—classes at 145
—getting started 142
—requirements for 146

Consistency 62, 64, 100
—for the older dog 134
Core vaccines 118
Coronavirus 118-119
Correction 97
Countrysides kennels 17
Crate 51, 59-60, 67, 92-93
—pads 52
Crying 60, 66, 94
Ctenocephalides canis **122**
Curly Pfeifer 13
Curly-Coated Retriever 10, 121
Cushing's disease 120
Dangers in the home 57-58
DEET 127
Degenerative joint disease 138
Demodex folliculoram **126**
Demodex mites 127
Dental care 81, 113, 115
—senior dog 139
Diabetes 120
Diet for senior dog 138
Digging 29
Dipylidium caninum **129**
Dirofilaria immitis **129**
Discipline 64, 96
Distemper 118-119
Dog clubs 143
Dog flea 122
Dominance 100
Down 95, 101
Down/stay 103
Dry baths 77
Ear
—cleaning 80
—mite infestation 80
Emergency care 131-132
English Water Spaniel 10
Epilepsy 120-121
Estrus 118
Events Calendar 146
Excessive chewing 30
Excessive thirst 71
Exercise 71
—pen 92
—puppy 72
—senior dog 138
External parasites 122-127
Eye
—care 80
—disorders 46, 120
Falk, John R. 35
Family meeting the puppy 59
Fear period 58, 60, 62
Feeding 46, 68-69
Fenced yard 58
Fiala, Jiri 24
Field Dog Stud Book 13
Field Spaniel 10
Field training 33

Field trials 15, 146
Finland 24
First aid 132-133
First night in new home 59
Fleas **122-123**, 124
Flyball 19, 153
Follicular dysplasia 120-121
Food 93
—bowls 51
—rewards 88, 106
—toxic to dogs 68
Ford, Linda 121
Fox River Valley 8
Genetic testing 45-46, 111
German Shorthaired Pointer 15
Getting started in showing 142
Giardia 119
Grapes 68
Gray wolf 10
Great Britain 25
Grinder for nails 78
Grooming 71-73, 75-78
Group competition 142, 146
Growth 72
Gum disease 113
Handler 140
Happy Hiram of Ty-Grim 14
Health
—adult 113
—benefits of dog ownership 27
—journal 59
—puppy 58, 111
—senior dog 115, 137
Heart disease 115
Heartworm 113, **129**, 130, **131**
Heat cycle 118
Heel 104, 106
Hepatitis 118-119
Heterodoxus spiniger **126**
Hinz, Karl 13
Hip dysplasia 46, 120, 138
Homemade toys 55
Hookworm **128**, **129**
House-training 51, 91, 94
—puppy needs 91
—schedule 90, 96
Hunting 15, 20, 30-32, 109
Hunting Retriever Club 20, 152-153
Hunting tests 20, 146, 151
Hypothyroidism 46, 120
Identification 46, 83
Infectious diseases 117
Insurance 58, 117
Internal parasites 128-131
Irish Water Spaniel 10, 121
Ixodes dammini **124-125**
Johnnie 22
Judges 144-145
Jumper agility titles 150

Jumping up 95
Junior Hunter 152
Junior Showmanship 147
Kennel Club, The 25, 140
Keoni 121
Kidney problems 115
Labrador Retriever 15
Lagimoniere, Beth 121
Leash 55, 97
—pulling on 105
Leave it 30
Leptospirosis 118-119
Lifespan 113
Little Brownie's Gunner Boy 16, 18
Louse 126
Lyme disease 118, 124
Macadamia nuts 68
Majors 144
Mammary cancer 118
Mange 125
Market hunters 8-9
Massage 137
Master Agility Champion 150
Master Agility Dog 150
Master Agility Excellent 150
Master Hunter 152
Microchip 46, 84
Miettinen, Maria 24
Miscellaneous Class 148
Misty 24
Mites 125
Morrison, Paul R. 16
Mosquitoes 127
Mounting 118
Nail clipping 72, 77-78
Name 99, 104
Narhi, Tiina 25
National Obedience Champion 148
Neutering 58, 113, 118, 120, 146
Night Hawks Sweet Chocolate 25
Nipping 65
Non-core vaccines 118
Non-slip retriever 153
North American Hunting Retriever Association 20, 151-153
Novice Agility 150
Novice Class 145
Nuts 68
Obedience 19, 30, 102, 106, 146-148, 153
Obesity 138
Off 95
Okay 101, 105
Open Agility 150
Open Class 145
Orthopedic Foundation for Animals 120
Orthopedic problems of senior dog 138

Osteochondritis dissecans 138
Other dogs 118
Other pets 90
Outdoor safety 58
Ovariohysterectomy 118
Ownership 49-50
—health benefits of 27
Pack animals 10, 63
Paper-training 91, 94-95
Parainfluenza 118
Parasites
—external 122-127
—internal 128-131
—preventives 122
Parent club 143, 146
Parvovirus 118-119
Patience 90
Pfeifer, Dr. F. J. 10, 13, 23
Physical characteristics 36
Playtime 103
Pointer 15
Poisons 55, 58, 68
Portuguese Water Dog 121
Positive reinforcement 59, 96-97, 99
Possessiveness 28
Practicing 102
—commands 100
Praise 89, 96, 106
Preventive care 111, 113, 115
Prostate problems 118
Pulling on leash 105
Punishment 67, 96-97
Puppy 44
—common problems 65
—establishing leadership 88
—exercise 72
—feeding 69
—first night in new home 59
—health 58, 111
—kindergarten training class 98
—meeting the family 59
—personality 50, 113
—selection 44, 47, 50, 111
—show quality 140-141
—socialization 27-28, 61
—supplies for 51
—teething 65
—training 60, 63, 88
Puppy Class 145
Pure-bred dogs 9, 37
Rabies 118-119
Racing 109
Raisins 68
Rally obedience 19, 153
Rawhides 54
Raz 25
Requirements for show 146
Reserve Winners Bitch 145
Reserve Winners Dog 145
Retriever field trials 151
Retrieving Certificate Tests 21, 34, 153

Rewards 89, 96-97, 106
—food 97
Rhabditis 129
Ripley's Believe It or Not! 22
Roaming 118
Robinson, Mike and Dorthea 17
Rope toys 54
Roundworm 128
Rutherford, Tom and Constance 15
Safety 52, 55, 68, 85, 92, 94, 103
—at home 56
—outdoors 58
Sarcoptes mites 125
Sarcoptes scabiei 125
Sarcoptic mange 125
Scanlan, Driscoll 13, 35
Scent attraction 96
Schedule 90
Scofield, John 13
Selecting a pup 47
Senior dog 113
—behavioral changes 135
—consistency 134
—dental care 139
—diet 69, 138
—exercise 138
—health 115
—signs of aging 135
—veterinary care 136
Senior Hunter 152
Shedding 30-31
Shelberg, Charles 13
Sherlock, John 13
Shopping for puppy needs 51
Show quality 140, 141
Shows
—costs of 141
Sit 99
Sit/stay 102
Smith, Louis 13
Socialization 27, 60-61, 63, 99, 113
—puppy 28
Soft toys 54
Sos, Josef 24
Spaniel Hunt Test 21, 153
Spaying 58, 113, 118, 146
Specials 145
Specialty show 143
Spisak, Barbara 17
Sporting dogs 109
Spot bath 77
Standard 37, 142
Stay 102, 104, 106
Stress 99
Supervision 64-65, 94
Surgery 118
Taenia pisiformis 130
Tangle 34
Tapeworm 129, 130
Tattoo 46, 84
Teeth 113

Teething period 65
Temperament 48-49
—evaluation 113
Testicular cancer 118
Therapy dog 109, 153
Thirst 71
Ticks 124-125
Timing 95, 104
Toxins 55, 58, 68
Toxocara canis 129
Toys 53, 66, 92, 94
Tracking 32, 109, 146
Training 26-28, 31, 64
—basic principles 88
—commands 100
—consistency in 62, 100
—early 63
—field 33, 155
—getting started 97
—importance of timing 95, 104
—puppy 60
—tips 64
Traveling 51, 87
Treats 59, 89, 97
—weaning off in training 106
Tricks 109
Ty-Grim kennels 17
Tyler, Thomas 13
Type 140-141
Types of shows 143
United Kennel Club 13-14, 19, 140, 152
United States Dog Agility Association 149
University of Missouri 121
Urine marking 118
Utility Dog 19, 147
Utility Dog Excellent 148
Vaccinations 46, 58-59, 62, 113, 117, 118
Veterinarian 54, 58, 113, 115-116
Veterinary insurance 117
Visiting the litter 50
Walker, Mrs. Helen Whitehouse 147
Water 70, 93
—bowls 51
—increased intake 71
West Nile virus 127
Westminster Kennel Club 14, 141
Whining 60, 66, 94
Wildemoor kennels 17
Winners Bitch 145
Winners Class 145
Winners Dog 145
Wisconsin 17
Wish N' Well Tarheel Marksman 141
Wolf 10
Wolf Valley 8
World War II 14
Yard 58
Yodel 29

My AWS

PUT YOUR PUPPY'S FIRST PICTURE HERE

Dog's Name _____

Date _____ Photographer _____